FROM
THE
NORTH

FROM THE NORTH

A Simple and
Modern Approach
to Authentic
Nordic Cooking

KATRÍN BJÖRK
Founder of Modern Wifestyle

PAGE STREET
PUBLISHING CO.

PAGE STREET
PUBLISHING CO.

First published in 2018 by

Page Street Publishing Co.

27 Congress Street, Suite 105

Salem, MA 01970

www.pagestreetpublishing.com

Distributed by Macmillan, sales in Canada by The Canadian Manda Group.

22   21   20   19   18   1   2   3   4   5

ISBN 13: 978-1-62414-530-8

ISBN-10: 1-62414-530-2

Library of Congress Control Number: 2017952212

Cover and book design by Page Street Publishing Co.

Photography copyright © 2018 by Katrín Björk

Printed and bound in China

FOR AMMA AND AFI.

I KNOW YOU WOULD HAVE BEEN SO PROUD IF YOU HAD LIVED TO SEE THIS BOOK
COME TO LIFE. YOU MIGHT NOT HAVE AGREED WITH ALL THE WILD PAIRINGS AND
STRANGE COMBINATIONS, BUT YOU WOULD HAVE LOVED EVERY SINGLE BITE,
I'M SURE OF IT.

INTRODUCTION—GJÖRIÐ ÞIÐ SVO VEL   8

FROM THE SEA—FISH & SHELLFISH   10

FROM THE HEATH—MEAT, GAME & FOWL   50

FROM THE GARDEN—SALADS & SIDES   82

FROM THE PAST— CURED & SMOKED DELICACIES   108

FROM THE PANTRY— PICKLES, PRESERVES & PATÉS   128

FROM THE OVEN—SOURDOUGH & LOAVES   146

FROM THE HEART— SWEET TREATS & DESSERTS   158

ABOUT THE AUTHOR   185

ACKNOWLEDGMENTS   186

INDEX   188

INTRODUCTION

GJÖRIÐ ÞIÐ SVO VEL

To grow up with a fishing grandpa, a farming grandma and a hunting father was a fortune that I didn't appreciate until years after moving away from Iceland, the icy island in the North where I was born. I took all of it for granted and never thought about what it meant to be this lucky, how precious it is to forage, to hunt and to coexist with nature—it was the norm to me and now I miss it terribly. Moving from a city to a small town in the Hudson Valley of New York and being closer to nature in my everyday life has brought back an urge to return to the basics.

When given the opportunity to write a cookbook, I didn't have to think long before saying yes and settling on the concept of Nordic cooking. For a long time I have wanted to share my memories and the childhood favorites that over the years I have adapted and developed and made my own.

After living in Copenhagen for 15 years and being married to a Dane, I have of course been inspired by Danish cooking and the wonders of the new Nordic scene, so mixed in with true Icelandic dishes you will find Danish classics and you will even find one Norwegian recipe and one Swedish; therefore, I allow myself to call this book Nordic and not Icelandic.

Everything was cooked from scratch in my childhood home. Nothing complicated or advanced, just humble food prepared simply. On summer camping trips we collected mushrooms and fried them in butter with wild arctic thyme. On weekends there were whole roasted geese and ptarmigans on the table, and on weekdays there was fresh fish from grandpa's boat and young lamb from the farm. On birthdays there was a large plate of flatbread with butter and smoked lamb or salmon right next to the chocolate cake.

It's been exciting to create new dishes from something so familiar and to push myself to elevate the well-known. I have stayed true to and have involved many of the main elements of Nordic cooking, such as smoking and curing, but in an easy and accessible way so everybody can follow along. I promise you, there is no need to build a smokehouse or dig an oven in the ground; it is all kitchen-safe.

Instead of cold-smoking meats, as is common in Iceland, I hot smoke other, more simple ingredients on my stove top, to bring the smoky flavor to your plate. I also cure a few things, both in traditional manner and in my own way, breaking a few rules and using ancient techniques for something new, while staying true to the flavor of the North.

Creating this book has brought back flavors I haven't tasted in years and it has been a beautiful—and quite frankly emotional—journey for me. I cooked and photographed part of this book at home in my mama's kitchen in Iceland and my family helped me gather ingredients that were far out of season. Berries and birds got pulled out of freezers all over Iceland for me to cook.

Almost every recipe and dish in this book can be paired to create an elegant meal, or you can cook multiple recipes for a Nordic buffet. You can mix and match, swap ingredients and cook this book from one end to another, all at once or one recipe at a time.

My hope is to inspire you, to create a feeling of hygge and to place you in my grandma's kitchen for a bowl of lamb broth or at a family feast with game and warm spices. But most of all, I want you to have fun and cook.

KATRINBJ.

A NOTE ON MEASUREMENTS: Hi metric measuring people. This book was initially written for the American market and therefore the main measurements are in pounds, ounces, quarts and spoons. You will find metric measurements in parentheses when needed. Sometimes the measurements in this book are so small that a conversion didn't make sense to me. For instance, a tablespoon of parsley equals 1 gram and I am assuming you are not a professional chef and therefore not in ownership of a super-precise kitchen scale, so I decided that it was better for you just to read the spoon measurements. The short version: Any spoon measurement that equals less than 15 grams still stands as teaspoons or tablespoons and no metrics are given. To help you wrap your head around it even better: 1 tbsp = 15 ml.

FROM THE SEA

FISH & SHELLFISH

After moving away from Iceland, I realized that not everybody grew up eating fresh fish multiple times a week and that, in general, people don't eat a lot of seafood at home. When I ask friends why they don't cook more fish, the most common answer is a shoulder shrug followed by a story about an unsuccessful fish dish cooked in the past.

As with most things, fish is best when fresh, wild and in season. It should always have a mild, fresh scent and never smell fishy. The color should be vibrant with no discoloration or brown edges. The flesh should be firm and moist with no separations, gaps or blood. If you are cooking a whole fish, the eyes should be bright and bulging, the flesh firm and shiny and the gills should be bright pink or red.

If you are new to cooking fish, start with my grandma's Icelandic Fishcakes with Cauliflower (page 30) and the Grilled Salmon Steaks with Pickled Lovage (page 45), and when your confidence starts to grow, go for the Whole Grilled Snapper (page 41). You will not regret it and it is much easier than you might think.

ARCTIC CHAR TARTARE

Arctic char is a cold-water fish in the salmon family with a flavor profile somewhere in between salmon and lake trout.

It is easy to crisp the skin of an arctic char, so if you get a piece with skin on, don't toss it, use it as garnish for the tartare or any other delicious fish dish you might be cooking.

YIELD: 4 SERVINGS AS AN APPETIZER OR 2 AS A MAIN COURSE

10 oz (285 g) arctic char

⅓ cucumber

1 tbsp fresh mint, minced

1 tbsp chives, minced

½ tbsp olive oil

½ tbsp vinegar

½ small lemon, juice and zest

Salt and pepper

¼ small fennel bulb

½ cup (120 ml) oil for frying

Several sprigs of dill

Remove the skin, then clean and devein the fish. Place the fish in the freezer for about 20 minutes so it is easier to slice. Then cut the chilled fish into ⅛-inch (3-mm) cubes.

Deseed and dice the cucumber and place in a bowl with the char, mint and chives.

Whisk together the olive oil, vinegar, a little lemon zest and 1 teaspoon of lemon juice, salt and pepper to taste, then pour the dressing over the tartare and toss to combine.

Finely slice the fennel. Fry half of it in hot oil for about 10 minutes or until golden. Sprinkle the fried fennel with salt and drizzle the fresh half with a few drops of lemon juice.

Place a spoonful of tartare on a pretty plate, top with both the fresh and fried fennel and decorate with a few sprigs of dill.

SCALLOP CEVICHE
WITH ELDERFLOWER

This is an elegant appetizer that takes no time to prepare but has both delicate flavor and beautiful texture. If you can get scallops in the shell I would definitely go for those, both for flavor and freshness but also because the shell makes a beautiful plate.

YIELD: 4 SERVINGS

8 large scallops

⅔ cup (160 ml) lime juice (approximately 5 limes)

½ tsp salt

½ cucumber, sliced

Fresh dill

Fresh mint

4 tsp elderflower cordial

Pepper

Remove the scallops from the shell and slice them thinly. If you are using frozen scallops it is a good idea to slice them before they thaw completely, as it is much easier to cut half-frozen than thawed fish!

Squeeze the limes and add ½ teaspoon of salt to the juice. Place the sliced scallops in the juice and let marinate for 20 to 30 minutes, or until firm but not rubbery. Take the scallop slices out of the juice but do not dry them, just let them drip off, letting a few drops of juice fall on the serving plate. Divide the scallops between four shells (or plates) and arrange along with cucumber slices, dill and mint. Pour 1 teaspoon of elderflower cordial over each plate and crack a little bit of black pepper over as well.

GRILLED WILD COLDWATER SHRIMP

WITH HAZELNUT MAYONNAISE

This easy peasy summery crowd pleaser is great as an appetizer or as part of a seafood feast.

You can peel the shrimp after grilling but they are also delicious to eat whole—the shells are crispy and flavorful. If you peel them, keep the shells and use them to make stock. I like to use coldwater shrimp for this recipe. Wild coldwater shrimp, or northern shrimp, are caught in the cold, clean North Atlantic Ocean. They are small and pink with firm flesh and lightly salted flavor and a sweet aftertaste. If your local seafood store doesn't have this type of shrimp, ask the fishmonger to order them for you!

YIELD: 2 SERVINGS

SHRIMP

1 lb (450 g) coldwater shrimp in shell

Olive oil

Salt and pepper

Slices of sourdough loaf

MAYONNAISE

1 handful hazelnuts

1 egg

½ cup (120 ml) neutral-tasting oil, such as sunflower or avocado

Salt and pepper

1 tsp lemon juice

4-6 lemon wedges

Preheat the oven to 375°F (190°C). Line a baking sheet with parchment paper.

Toss the shrimp with some olive oil, salt and pepper. Grill on high heat for a few minutes or until starting to char. Drizzle the bread with some olive oil and throw it on the grill and let toast.

Place the hazelnuts on the parchment-lined baking sheet and toast in the oven for 8 to 10 minutes, or until fragrant and darkened. Rub the hot hazelnuts together between your hands or in a kitchen towel to remove their skins. Chop them into a coarse meal, by hand or with a food processor.

To make the mayonnaise, it is easiest to use an immersion blender, but you can also whisk by hand if you do not have one. Crack the egg into a tall container and add the oil. Place the immersion blender in all the way to the bottom. Blend on high until you see the mayonnaise forming, then slowly move the blender upward (while blending) and the mayonnaise will come together. Add the chopped hazelnuts, salt, pepper and lemon juice and blend until homogeneous.

Serve the shrimp with grilled sourdough slices, hazelnut mayo, lemon wedges and tons of napkins—this is an eat-with-your-hands kind of dish! You can dip the shrimp in the mayo, or spread the mayo on the bread—it's up to you!

PACIFIC OYSTERS

WITH BLUEBERRY MIGNONETTE

Few things are as elegant as a bed of fresh oysters served as an appetizer or as an afternoon delight with a glass of champagne on a sunny summer day. Opening oysters is a practice-makes-perfect kind of thing, but it isn't as hard as they say. Just wear a glove, be confident and the oyster will obey.

YIELD: 6 SERVINGS, AS AN APPETIZER

¼ cup (60 ml) sherry vinegar

¼ cup (60 ml) white wine vinegar

2 shallots, minced

½ cup (85 g) fresh blueberries

¼ cup parsley

½ tsp freshly cracked black pepper

2 dozen Pacific oysters

Make the vinaigrette first. Stir the vinegars and shallots together in a bowl. Purée the blueberries and parsley in a food processor and add to the vinegar. Add cracked black pepper to taste.

When you shuck your oysters wear gloves to prevent cutting yourself. Place an oyster in one gloved hand with the cup-shaped side down and the hinge (the pointy end with the muscle that connects the top and bottom shell) toward you. Scrub any grit off the oyster with a brush, then insert a thick bladed oyster knife 45 degrees downward into the hinge if you can, or go in from the side. Twist the knife slightly until you feel the hinge pop and then run the blade around to the other side. Be careful not to tip the oyster or you will lose all the lovely juices on the inside. Separate the oyster meat from the bottom shell so they will be ready to slurp. Arrange open oysters on a bed of ice and keep chilled until ready to serve. Open oysters will keep for a few days, on ice and in a very cold refrigerator.

Spoon vinaigrette over the oysters and then slurp. They are best with a glass of bubbly!

NOTE: When buying oysters, make sure they are alive. All the shells should be closed but if they are not, try lightly tapping an open shell on the counter. If it immediately shuts, the oyster is still alive and fine to eat, if it doesn't it is dead and inedible. Fresh oysters should smell like the crisp air by the sea—if they smell fishy they are not fresh. They should also feel heavy when laying in your palm—if not, the seawater has dried up and the oyster is no longer fresh.

KRÄFTSKIVA

CRAYFISH PARTY

If you have ever visited Sweden in August, you have probably been to a crayfish party: A festive gathering of family and friends where party hats, bibs and stacks of napkins are all equally necessary. It is also a party where heavy drinking and singing are the norm. Fun times for sure!

Crayfish or crawfish live in freshwater and are closely related to lobster, sometimes even called freshwater lobster. There is delicious sweet meat in the tails and they are best eaten with your hands. If you ask a person from Louisiana, they will tell you to serve 4 pounds (2 kg) per person for a full meal, but since in Sweden we serve bread, cheese and mayonnaise on the side, 1½ to 2 pounds (700 to 900 g) is more than plenty.

YIELD: 2 SERVINGS

CRAYFISH

4 quarts (4 L) water

¼ cup (70 g) salt

3 tbsp (40 g) sugar

1 bunch fresh dill

Several dill blossoms

4 lbs (2 kg) crayfish (around 60 pieces)

Bring the water, salt, sugar, dill and dill blossoms to a boil and let boil for 5 minutes. Remove the dill and blossoms and set aside. Make sure the water is at a rolling boil before you add the live crayfish. Add one crayfish at a time, one right after the other. Make sure you keep the water at a rolling boil so the crayfish die instantly when hitting the water. Work in batches (10 crayfish at a time) and let boil for 4 minutes before removing from the water.

After you have boiled all the crayfish, remove the pot from the heat and place the crayfish back in the water along with the dill and dill blossoms. Let steep for 3 to 4 hours or even overnight.

(continued)

KRÄFTSKIVA
CRAYFISH PARTY (CONTINUED)

MAYONNAISE

2 large egg yolks

1 tbsp lemon juice

1 tbsp white wine vinegar

1 tbsp Dijon mustard

½ tsp salt + more to taste

1 cup (240 ml) neutral oil, such as sunflower, avocado or peanut

1 tbsp finely chopped dill

SIDES

6 lemons, halved

1 bunch dill

Sourdough loaf

Comté or Gruyère (or other hard, nutty cheese)

Whisking by hand, or using a blender or a food processor, combine the egg yolks, lemon juice, vinegar, mustard and salt. Start adding the oil, one or two drops at a time, then slowly ease into pouring more freely, keeping the stream thin and steady. When you have added all the oil and the mayonnaise is thick and glossy, add some more salt and pepper to taste and fold in the dill.

Swedish crayfish are served cold with mayonnaise, lemons, some more dill, nice bread, flavorful cheese and plenty of beer or snaps on the side.

NOTE: Snaps is a type of Scandinavian alcohol (for example akvavit or aquavit) usually brewed with caraway seeds, dill or other natural flavor. It is served in a shot glass at gatherings of family and friends during lunch or dinner. It is very popular during Christmas and other holidays.

LOBSTER ROLL

WITH FENNEL SLAW

Lobster rolls are for sure an American phenomenon and they are not at all known in Scandinavia. But they should be! So, I came up with a Scandi version of the classic and I have to say, I really, really like it!

I like to serve my lobster roll with a hot bun and hot lobster, like I would a hot dog, but it is of course just as delicious when served cold.

YIELD: 8 SERVINGS

BRIOCHE

2 tbsp (25 g) sugar

¾ cup (180 ml) water (98–100°F [37–38°C])

2 tsp yeast

3 cups (400 g) tipo 00 flour (or bread flour)

1 tsp salt

3 eggs, divided

3 tbsp (45 g) butter, room temperature

Preheat the oven to 375°F (190°C). Grease a baking sheet.

Dissolve the sugar in the warm water, then add the yeast and let it sit for 10 minutes. Stir together the flour and salt in a large bowl, then add the yeast mixture and stir well. Whisk two eggs together, then add half to the dough and stir well. Add the other half and stir again. Then crumble in the butter and knead the dough for 10 minutes or until you have elastic and shiny dough. The dough will be super sticky but don't give up and don't get tempted to add more flour—it will come together, I promise.

Let the dough rest in the bowl, covered with plastic wrap, for 60 minutes.

Form the dough into 8 hotdog buns and place 1 inch (2.5 cm) apart on a greased baking sheet and let them rise under a damp kitchen towel for 1 hour.

Whisk the last egg in a small bowl, then brush onto the buns. Bake the buns for 15 to 18 minutes.

(continued)

LOBSTER ROLL

WITH FENNEL SLAW (CONTINUED)

LOBSTER

2 tbsp water

2 sticks (230 g) butter

3 garlic cloves, crushed

10 (4-oz [115-g]) lobster tails

TOPPINGS

½ small fennel bulb

1 green apple

1 tbsp finely chopped dill

4 oz (115 g) sunchokes

½ cup (120 ml) peanut oil for frying

DRESSING

½ cup (125 g) skyr

¼ tsp minced fresh chili

1 tsp lemon juice

Several drops liquid smoke (optional)

Salt and pepper

Remove the raw lobster from the shell and keep chilled.

Bring 2 tablespoons of water to a boil in a saucepan over medium-low heat, then add 1 tablespoon of butter, whisking constantly. When melted, add another tablespoon of butter and when that one has melted add the garlic. Keep adding butter a little at a time, while whisking, until you have added it all and you have a thick sauce. Make sure that the butter never boils; if it does, it will separate. If you have a thermometer, I highly recommend you use it to help you keep the beurre monté somewhere between 160 and 185°F (70 and 85°C).

Working in batches (2 to 3 tails at a time, depending on the size of your pot) poach the lobster tails for 6 to 7 minutes, or until they have reached 140 to 145°F (60 to 63°C). Cut each tail into 2 to 3 pieces.

Thinly slice or shred the fennel and apple, add the dill and toss to combine.

Peel the sunchokes and slice into paper-thin slices, using a mandoline or food processor. Heat the peanut oil to 375°F (190°C) and fry the sunchokes for a few minutes, or until crisp. Season with salt to taste.

Stir the skyr, chili, lemon juice and liquid smoke together, adding salt and pepper to taste.

Assemble the lobster rolls by putting the dressing on the buns, then adding lobster (a few drops of butter won't hurt), fresh slaw and crispy sunchokes on top.

NOTE: If you have my Smoked Skyr (see page 120) on hand, use that in the pressing and skip the liquid smoke.

CRISPY FLOUNDER

WITH SWEET ONIONS ON DANISH RYE

This is my modern version of a Danish classic, simply called fish fillet. Traditionally, it is served with a bright yellow remoulade dressing but here you have a more deconstructed version that still gives you crispy fish, along with something sweet and something tangy.

YIELD: 2 SERVINGS

1 yellow onion

2 tbsp (30 g) butter, divided

1 tsp sugar

2 tbsp (30 ml) balsamic vinegar

Salt and pepper

1 lb (450 g) flounder fillets

1 egg

¾ cup (80 g) almond flour

Danish Rye Bread (or other dark and savory bread), sliced (page 155)

Dijon mustard

4 radishes

Small capers

Fennel fronds

½ lemon

Finely slice the onion and add it to a pan with 1 tablespoon of butter and a pinch of salt. Let cook over low-medium heat for 15 minutes, stirring occasionally. Sprinkle the sugar over the onion and let it caramelize for 10 more minutes before deglazing the pan with the vinegar. Let simmer until the vinegar has evaporated.

While the onion is cooking, generously salt and pepper the flounder fillets. Lightly whisk the egg in a shallow bowl then dip the fish first in egg, then coat with almond flour. Fry in 1 tablespoon of butter over medium-high heat for a few minutes on each side, or until golden.

"Butter" the bread with a thin layer of Dijon mustard, place the fish on top and garnish with onions, radishes, capers and fennel fronds. Serve with a lemon wedge on the side and ice cold beer.

FRIED COD CHEEKS

WITH BAKED ROOT VEGETABLE CRISPS

In small pockets right below the eye, you find the most tender and sweet part of the fish. Most cheeks, cod included, are the ideal size for frying and you do not have to cut or prep anything, they are perfect just the way they are.

In Iceland, you can always find cheeks at the fishmonger's but because they are not common everywhere in the world you might want to call ahead and put in an order.

YIELD: 2 SERVINGS

CHEEKS

2 cups (500 ml) peanut oil

1 lb (450 g) cod cheeks

Salt and pepper

¾ cup (95 g) flour

¼ tsp smoked paprika

1 cup (240 ml) beer

ROOT VEGETABLES

14 oz (400 g) rutabaga

14 oz (400 g) beets

3 tbsp olive oil

Salt and pepper

DIPPING SAUCE

¾ cup (185 g) skyr

½ lemon, juice and zest

Handful dill, finely chopped

Salt and pepper

Preheat the oven to 375°F (190°C). In a deep fryer or deep skillet, heat the peanut oil to 350 to 375°F (175 to 190°C).

Rinse the cod cheeks under cold water and pat them dry, then sprinkle with salt and pepper.

Stir the flour, smoked paprika, and a little bit of salt and pepper together, then slowly whisk in the beer. Dip one cheek at a time into the batter, let the batter drip off, then transfer directly to the oil and let them fry until golden, 3 to 4 minutes.

Thinly slice the rutabaga and beets, arrange them in a single layer on a baking sheet, drizzle with olive oil, salt and pepper. Bake for 15 to 20 minutes, flipping the slices over midway through the baking time.

Whisk together the skyr, lemon juice and zest and finely chopped dill. Season with salt and pepper to taste.

ICELANDIC FISHCAKES

WITH CAULIFLOWER

This recipe is close to my heart, as it is my grandma's. It is a simple and no fuss kind of recipe, but it is bulletproof—as long as you are using fresh fish. This is also a great recipe to build on, add to and make your very own. These fishcakes are excellent for freezing so make a double batch. Reheat them in butter with some grated nutmeg, or serve them cold on a piece of Danish Rye Bread (page 155).

YIELD: 4 SERVINGS

CELERY LEAVES

12 celery leaves

½ cup (120 ml) vinegar

½ cup (120 ml) water

1 tbsp sugar

Salt

FISHCAKES

1 lb (450 g) cod fillets

2 small yellow onions, quartered

2 eggs

3 tbsp (30 g) potato starch

3 tbsp (23 g) flour

2 tsp salt

½ stick (55 g) butter

CAULIFLOWER

½ cauliflower head

½ stick (55 g) butter

Pinch of nutmeg

Fennel fronds for garnish

Start by pickling the celery leaves. If the leaves are soggy or soft, place them in ice water for a few minutes to crisp them up. Whisk together the vinegar, water and sugar, season with a pinch of salt and place the leaves in the marinade. Let sit for 20 minutes.

Wash and dry the fish, then place in a food processor along with the quartered onions, eggs, potato starch, flour and salt. Pulse until creamy and fluffy. Using two tablespoons, form the fish mixture into approximately 16 quenelles (elongated egg shapes).

Working in batches to avoid crowding the pan, fry the fishcakes in the butter over medium heat until nicely browned and cooked through, 3 to 4 minutes each side. Remove from the pan and keep warm until serving.

Cut the cauliflower into florets. Keep some whole and thinly slice a few of them. Using the pan you cooked the fish in, and without wiping it down, add the butter and let it brown slightly. Grate the nutmeg over the butter and then fry half of the cauliflower for a few minutes. Keep the other half of the cauliflower fresh and as is.

Place the fishcakes on a plate along with a few pickled celery leaves, fresh and fried cauliflower and fennel fronds. Spoon generously with the nutmeg butter from the pan.

NIGHT SALTED COD

WITH GRILLED CUCUMBER AND FAVA BEANS

I probably had salted cod (baccalau) twice a week my entire childhood. It was inexpensive and salting the fish was a great way to extend its shelf life. During my twenties, I didn't touch salted cod with my little finger, that's how much I had had of it as a child and teenager. But, I am ready for it again, although I do prefer it in smaller amounts and in a lighter version than what I shoveled down growing up.

YIELD: 2 SERVINGS

SALTED COD

1 lb (450 g) fresh, wild cod fillets

1½ oz (40 g) salt

2 cups (450 ml) water

2 cups (450 ml) milk

1 garlic clove

1 bay leaf

VEGGIES

½ cucumber

1½ lbs (700 g) fava beans in pods

3 tbsp (45 g) butter

1 garlic clove, crushed

1 tbsp fresh dill

Several blackberries

Black pepper

To brine the cod, start 8 to 12 hours prior to serving the fish. Dissolve the salt in water, place the fish in the salted water, cover and place the bowl in the refrigerator for 8 to 12 hours.

Bring the milk, garlic and bay leaf to a boil in a saucepan large enough to hold the fish. Remove from the heat and poach the fish in the hot milk, with the lid on, for 5 minutes or until tender.

Shave the cucumber into long strips with a vegetable peeler and grill on a lightly greased grill pan over high heat for a couple of minutes or until nicely charred.

Shell the fava beans and blanch them in lightly salted, boiling water for 60 seconds. Drain and allow the beans to cool. When the beans are cool enough to handle, peel off the thin casing/skin from every bean.

Melt the butter in a small saucepan over medium heat, add garlic and dill and let the beans poach in the butter for a couple of minutes or until tender. Keep basting the beans while they are in the butter so they cook evenly.

Arrange cucumber strips, fish and blackberries on a plate, spoon fava beans and a generous amount of the dill butter onto each plate and crack some black pepper over. This dish is great served with roasted potatoes.

PAN-FRIED FLOUNDER

WITH BERRY BUTTER AND HERBS

Cooking fish with the skin on gives you a great opportunity to add texture and crunch. Salty, crispy fish skin is also delicious—kind of like bacon, just better if you ask me.

YIELD: 2 SERVINGS

BERRY BUTTER

½ stick (55 g) butter, room temperature

1 tbsp sour cream

1 tbsp blueberries

1 tbsp red currants (or raspberries)

FLOUNDER

2 flounder fillets, skin on

1 tsp salt

1 tsp pepper

2 cloves garlic

2 tbsp (30 ml) neutral oil, such as avocado, vegetable or peanut oil, or butter for frying

2 tbsp dill

2 tbsp parsley

2 tsp blueberry salt

One hour prior to cooking, wash and pat dry the flounder fillets. Then place them skin side up on a plate and place in the refrigerator for 60 minutes. This will help you get perfect, crispy skin.

While the fish is chilling, with an electric mixer or strong arm, whip the butter until smooth and fluffy. Add the sour cream and whip some more. Then add the berries and whip to combine for a few seconds; you want a few of the berries to break up and some to stay whole. Set aside until ready to serve.

Season the flounder fillets with salt and pepper. Peel and crush the garlic cloves and add them along with oil to a pan. Heat the oil on medium-high and fry the fish, skin side down, for 4 to 5 minutes or until the flesh is firm and cooked. There is no need to turn the fish—this will give you a crispy skin and delicate flesh. Spoon a little of the garlic oil from the pan over the fish while frying.

Chop the dill and parsley and mix together with the blueberry salt.

Serve the fillets whole, with berry butter and a sprinkle of the herb and blueberry salt mixture. This buttery flounder pairs well with newly harvested potatoes.

NOTE: Blueberry salt is available online or in specialty stores.

BAKED COD
WITH FENNEL AND FOAM

Foam is the culinary child of the 1990s and it has been overused at restaurants since, but I still find it elegant and a nice touch for a dish when having guests over.

I use smoked salt in this recipe; you can get it online and in many specialty stores, but you can easily replace it with regular salt and add a few drops of liquid smoke instead. Or you can lose the smokiness all together, that's up to you.

YIELD: 2 SERVINGS

FOAM

½ large fennel bulb

½ tbsp olive oil

1 cup (240 ml) milk

1 cup (240 ml) water

Pinch of salt

1 tsp soy lecithin

PURÉE

1 large fennel bulb

2 tbsp (30 g) butter

1 tbsp natural sour cream (no stabilizer added)

Salt and pepper

FISH

1 lb (450 g) fresh cod fillets

Smoked salt

Black pepper

Olive oil

Preheat the oven to 350°F (175°C).

Make the base for the foam by first washing then cutting ½ of a fennel bulb into small pieces, stalks and fronds included. Place the fennel in a pan and sauté in the olive oil for about 10 minutes over medium heat until the fennel has softened and has started to brown slightly. Pour the milk, water and a pinch of salt over the fennel, bring to a boil, cover and let simmer for 20 minutes. Remove from the heat and let steep for 30 minutes. Add all of the cooled mixture to a blender or food processor and blend to a purée and then strain through a cheesecloth. You should have about ½ cup (120 ml) of fennel liquid. Set aside until right before it is time to serve.

To make the fennel purée, take the remaining fennel bulb, slice the white part and set aside the stalks and fronds. Place in a pot of boiling, lightly salted water. Let boil for 10 minutes or until the fennel is tender. Drain the fennel and add it to a bowl together with the butter and sour cream. Blend with an immersion blender or food processor until smooth. Season with salt and pepper to taste.

Season the cod with smoked salt and black pepper and drizzle with some olive oil. Place in an ovenproof dish with a few sprigs of fennel fronds on top. Bake until tender, about 12 minutes.

Right before serving, add the soy lecithin to the fennel liquid and whisk with an immersion blender until bubbly foam forms. If you do not have lecithin you can serve the liquid as jus instead.

Spread the purée on plates, place the fish on top and spoon the foam over.

PAN-FRIED HADDOCK

WITH ROSEMARY AND RHUBARB

When testing this recipe, I stopped by the house of an elderly lady I know to get some rhubarb from her garden. When I told her I was planning on grilling it she laughed and said she'd probably eaten 100 pounds of rhubarb in her lifetime but not once had she thought about grilling it. Here is the thing: Rhubarb is tangy and super hard when uncooked and is usually used for baked, sugary desserts, but I thought to myself, why not cook it to make it soft but keep it tangy and have it replace the lemon that is usually served with fish? And it worked. Give it a try!

YIELD: 2 SERVINGS

FISH

1 rosemary sprig

1 lb (450 g) haddock loins
(or cod loins)

Flour, for dusting

Salt and pepper

2 tbsp (30 ml) neutral oil, such as
safflower or sunflower

ROSEMARY

6 tbsp (90 ml) neutral oil, such
as peanut

4 rosemary sprigs

RHUBARB

2 rhubarb stalks

1 tbsp olive oil

Pinch of salt

BUTTER

½ stick (55 g) butter, at room
temperature

Handful parsley

For the fish, take the leaves off the rosemary stalk and chop them finely. Dust the fish with flour, chopped rosemary and salt and pepper to taste. Fry in the oil for 4 to 5 minutes each side over medium heat (10 minutes in total per 1-inch [2.5-cm] thickness is a good rule of thumb).

For the rosemary, pour 6 tablespoons (90 ml) of oil in a small pot and heat up to 350 to 375°F (175 to 190°C). Drop the whole sprigs of rosemary into the oil and let them crisp up. It only takes a few seconds for them to be ready so keep a close eye on them.

Drizzle the rhubarb with olive oil and a little salt. Grill on medium-high heat on a grill pan for a few minutes or until softened. Turn once or twice.

Whip the butter with the roughly chopped parsley.

Divide the fish between two plates and top with rhubarb and rosemary. Serve with a dollop of parsley butter, fingerling potatoes, barley or a green salad.

GRILLED WHOLE SNAPPER

Grilling a fish whole is probably the easiest way to prepare it and it is such a unique eating experience. The crispness of the skin and flakiness of the meat is an unbeatable texture combination.

This meal is simple but is meant to be eaten slowly—you have to be careful of bones—but practice makes perfect. For a light meal, half a fish per person is plenty but if you have a hungry crowd make a whole fish per person and use any leftovers to make a creamy fish salad the day after.

YIELD: 2–4 SERVINGS

2 red snappers, scaled and gutted

Salt and pepper

6 sprigs marjoram

4 sprigs flat-leaved parsley

Several celery or lovage leaves

1 lemon, sliced

Olive oil

Season the fish cavities with salt and pepper then stuff each cavity with marjoram sprigs, parsley, celery leaves and 2 to 3 lemon slices. Rub the outside of the snapper generously with olive oil and season with salt and pepper.

Heat a grill (or a grill pan) and grill the fish on high heat for 7 minutes per side. The fish will let go of the grill and you can easily flip it over when cooked through. If the fish sticks to the grill try giving it a couple more minutes and see if it does let go on its own (if not, you probably didn't use enough oil and will need to carefully scrape it off the grill).

Serve with a tomato salad and a chilled glass of bubbly rosé.

MONKFISH

WITH BEET DRESSING

Monkfish is one of the ugliest creatures on the planet, but it totally makes up for that in taste. The fillets or tails are often slimy looking but don't let that scare you, the flesh is meaty and has a lobster-like texture and flavor, which is why monkfish is often called "poor-man's lobster."

YIELD: 2 SERVINGS

BEET DRESSING

¾ cup (100 g) diced beet

½ red onion

1 tsp minced chili pepper

1 tbsp (21 g) honey

1 tbsp lemon juice

½ cup (125 g) skyr

FISH

Salt and pepper

1 lb (450 g) monkfish

Flour

Butter or neutral oil such as avocado or sunflower for frying

SALAD

½ cucumber

5 radishes

½ red onion

Small handful parsley

1 tsp white wine vinegar

1 tbsp olive oil

Make the dressing by placing beet, onion, chili, honey, lemon juice and skyr in a food processor. Process until the beets and onion are minced; the dressing will be slightly grainy. You will not need all of the dressing for this recipe; store leftover dressing in the refrigerator and eat on salad or grilled meat, or mix it into hummus.

Salt and pepper the fish, dust it with flour and fry for 4 minutes on each side in oil or butter over medium heat.

Thinly slice the cucumber, radishes and red onion and chop the parsley. Toss together with vinegar and olive oil.

Spoon the beet dressing on a plate, then place the fish and salad neatly on top.

GRILLED SALMON STEAKS
WITH PICKLED LOVAGE

Salmon steaks are not only beautiful when plated, they are easy to cook because they are all the same thickness, unlike fillets, which are thinner at one end.

Salmon is a fatty fish, so you can go nuts with the spices. Here you get sweetness from the sugar, a little heat from the smoked paprika and a punch of freshness from the pickled herb.

YIELD: 2 SERVINGS

LOVAGE

1 tbsp sugar

½ cup (120 ml) apple cider vinegar

½ cup (120 ml) water

Handful or two of lovage leaves

SALMON

1 tsp salt

½ tsp pepper

1 tsp brown sugar

½ tsp smoked paprika

1 tbsp olive oil

2 salmon steaks (1 to 1½ inches [2.5 to 3.5 cm] thick)

To pickle the lovage, dissolve the sugar in the vinegar and water and then add the leaves. Let the mixture sit for 30 to 60 minutes at room temperature.

Mix the salt, pepper, brown sugar, smoked paprika and olive oil together in a small bowl. Rub it on the salmon steaks and grill on medium-high heat for 4 to 6 minutes per side. You can also do this in a grill pan if you do not have access to a grill.

Serve with pickled lovage on top and crispy potatoes or boiled barley on the side.

NOTE: If you cannot find lovage you can use celery leaves instead, they are quite similar in taste and texture.

BLUE MUSSELS

WITH BEER

When eating blue mussels, I love using the empty shells as utensils. I know it might sound childish, but I truly love to slurp the broth with an empty shell and to use two half-shells as tongs to eat the meat. It somehow becomes more authentic this way and you automatically eat slower.

Mussels take time to clean and prep but the cook time is fast and they are perfect for serving a large group.

YIELD: 2 SERVINGS

2 lbs (1 kg) blue mussels

2 tbsp (30 g) butter

1 tbsp olive oil

2 shallots, chopped

4 garlic cloves, minced

½ fennel, thinly sliced

1 tsp chili flakes

12 oz (350 ml) Einstök White Ale, or any other white ale

1 tbsp cognac

Salt and pepper

Fresh parsley, chopped

Throw away any mussels with cracked shells, then rinse (but do not soak) the rest in cold water and remove all wire-like beards with your hands, scissors or a sponge. Tap all open mussels lightly onto the kitchen counter; if they close they are good to go, if not, throw them away.

Melt the butter and olive oil in a large pot and sauté the shallots, garlic, fennel and chili flakes for about 7 minutes over medium heat. Add the beer and bring to a boil.

Add the clean mussels to the pot and steam with lid on for 5 to 7 minutes. Gently shake the pot a few times during cooking.

Remove the mussels from the pot with a slotted spoon and set aside while you add some more flavor to the broth. Make sure to discard any shells that did not open during steaming. Add the cognac, salt and pepper to taste to the broth and bring to a quick boil.

Add the mussels back to the broth, sprinkle with fresh parsley and serve immediately with green salad, bread and/or french fries on the side.

ICELANDIC LANGOUSTINE BISQUE

WITH COGNAC

This is an Icelandic classic and every family and restaurant on the island have their own special recipe. It's salty and rich and absolutely delicious. Many Icelanders serve the bisque as an appetizer on Christmas Eve, but I find it a little too rich for that, so I serve it as a main course with a nice piece of sourdough bread on the side.

YIELD: 4 SERVINGS

2 lbs (1 kg) langoustine tails, shell on

3 tbsp (45 ml) olive oil

2 carrots, minced

2 stalks celery, minced

1 large onion, minced

1 garlic clove, minced

2 tbsp (33 g) tomato paste

4 cups (1 L) water

6 cups (1.5 L) fish stock

5 tbsp (70 g) butter

½ cup (60 g) flour

1 cup (240 L) heavy cream

Salt and pepper

A splash of cognac

Parsley for garnish

Shell the fish and place the meat in the refrigerator while preparing the stock.

Heat the olive oil in a large pot and fry the shells over medium-high heat until slightly browned and fragrant, about 5 to 7 minutes. Add the carrots, celery, onion and garlic, cook for 5 more minutes, then add the tomato paste. Stir well, then add the water and fish stock. Bring to a boil and skim the froth off the top. Lower the heat and let the stock simmer on low for 2½ to 3½ hours.

Strain carefully into a clean container; you might even want to do this a couple of times to get the clearest soup. Set the broth aside while you make a roux to thicken the soup. Start by washing the pot then melt the butter over medium heat. Add the flour and stir constantly until combined and slightly browned. Add the strained stock to the pot and cook until thickened, approximately 5 minutes. Add the heavy cream and season with salt and pepper.

About 5 minutes before serving, add the cognac and langoustine tails and, on medium–low heat, cook until the langoustine are heated through, a few minutes. Do not let the soup boil. Sprinkle with parsley for garnish.

FROM THE HEATH

MEAT, GAME & FOWL

I am a total lamb snob and I am not ashamed to admit it. In Iceland, lambs are born in the spring, then they wander the heath, eating berries and flowers for 3 to 4 months, before being slaughtered, fat and happy.

When choosing lamb, it is a good idea to ask your butcher how old the lamb was when slaughtered. Even though the definition of a lamb is a sheep under a year old, you do not want your lamb to be much older than 4 to 6 months. After that it will taste wool-like and that is a flavor you want to avoid!

In this chapter, you will find recipes for reindeer and whole wild birds, both traditional and more modern lamb dishes and classic Danish and Icelandic holiday meals. If in doubt about what to try first, I highly recommend the Leg of Lamb with Rosemary, Garlic and Berry Marinade (page 61) and if feeling adventurous, go for the Reindeer Tartare with Crowberries (page 54).

BROTH OF LAMB
WITH RUTABAGA

This is my absolute favorite dish from the Icelandic kitchen!

Traditionally, this soup is as rustic as it gets and is served as a stew. I am pretty sure that my grandma would roll her eyes if she saw my clarified version of the dish. If you feel like making the "real" version then skip the steps where I clarify the broth and don't roast your rutabaga in the oven, just boil it with the soup. Then turn the soup into a stew by adding a handful of rice for thickening.

YIELD: 4 SERVINGS

SOUP

Salt and pepper

2 lbs (1 kg) lamb shoulder

2 tbsp (30 g) butter

2 carrots

2 parsnips

1 leek

5 cups (1.25 L) water

Lamb bouillon (stock cube), optional

RUTABAGA

12 oz (350 g) rutabaga, divided

Olive oil

Salt and pepper

Preheat the oven to 375°F (190°C).

Salt and pepper the meat and brown it in some butter in a cast iron pot over medium–high heat, 4 to 5 minutes each side. While the meat browns, finely chop the carrots, parsnips and leek. When the meat has gotten a nice color on both sides, add the vegetables to the pot and mix everything together. Add the water and bring to a boil.

Let simmer for at least 1 hour. Taste the broth and if you think it doesn't have enough meaty flavor you can add a little lamb stock to help it along (my grandma would not approve though!).

If you would like to follow the traditional way of cooking this soup/ stew add the rutabaga in big chunks directly to the soup and cook until tender. My grandma also added potatoes and a handful of rice to thicken the soup and turn it into a stew. But, if you are feeling fancy (as I was when I took this picture) strain the broth a couple of times through a cheesecloth (but don't discard the solids).

Cut half of the rutabaga into cubes and place in an ovenproof pan, drizzle with olive oil and season with salt and pepper. Bake for 20 minutes, or until tender (cooking time will depend on the size of your cubes). Slice the other half of the rutabaga with a mandoline for paper-thin slices.

Place a piece of meat onto a plate, put a scoop of vegetables on top, then roasted rutabaga cubes and fresh rutabaga on top of everything. Carefully spoon the broth over the meat and vegetables. This fancy version will give you more textures, whereas the old-school method gives you a more powerful flavor. I leave the decision to you.

REINDEER TARTARE
WITH CROWBERRIES

Reindeer is an Icelandic classic and the wait list for hunting these beautiful and tasty animals is long. Every year there is a lottery for the few animals allowed to be hunted and families sit with crossed fingers in anticipation, waiting to find out whether or not there will be reindeer on the table for the holidays.

Both reindeer and crowberries can be hard to come by, so you can easily replace them with venison and blueberries.

YIELD: 4 SERVINGS
AS AN APPETIZER

¾ lb (350 g) reindeer (venison) fillet

2 shallots

5 juniper berries

¼ green apple

¼ cup (15 g) flat-leafed parsley

¼ cup (37 g) crowberries

1 (wild, if possible, see page 115) egg yolk

1 tsp mustard

Several drops sherry vinegar

Salt and pepper

Handful almonds, finely chopped

Place the meat in the freezer for 30 minutes before cutting it into small cubes. You do not want to mince your meat; it's lovely to have some texture in the tartare, but be careful not to make the cubes too large either.

Mince the shallots and juniper berries, cut the apples into cubes the same size as the meat, chop the parsley and keep the crowberries whole or halved depending on their size. Place in a bowl along with the meat.

Whisk the egg yolk, mustard and vinegar together and add salt and pepper to taste. Dress the tartare with the dressing then divide between 4 plates and sprinkle the almonds over each plate.

NOTE: If you have Smoked Almonds (page 123), they are a wonderful topping for the tartare.

REINDEER MEATBALLS

WITH MUSHROOMS

Meatballs are easy to make and perfect for feeding a crowd. For a lighter version of this dish, serve the meatballs without the gravy, with fresh arugula salad and rhubarb compote on the side. The rhubarb compote is sweet and almost dessert-like but goes so nicely with the earthiness of the mushrooms and the gamey flavor of the meatballs. In both Iceland and Sweden, it is very common to eat sweet jam with meat and fish; the sweetness balances the curing, salting and smoking usually done to preserve the meat.

YIELD: 4 SERVINGS

MEATBALLS

1 lb (450 g) ground reindeer or venison

1 egg

1 small yellow onion, finely chopped

2 cloves garlic, minced

2 tbsp chopped walnuts

3 tbsp bread crumbs

½ tsp thyme (dried)

½ tsp rosemary (dried)

½ tsp sage (dried)

3 juniper berries, ground

Salt and pepper

2 tbsp (30 g) butter

GRAVY

8 oz (225 g) mushrooms (chanterelles and porcinis are great)

Salt and pepper

½ tsp crushed angelica seeds (or fennel seeds)

2 tbsp (16 g) flour

3 tbsp (45 g) butter

½ cup (240 ml) heavy cream

1 tbsp (20 g) rhubarb compote or other jam

In a large bowl, mix all the meatball ingredients except the butter. Form small meatballs, using approximately 1 tablespoon of meat mixture per ball. Melt the butter in a pan over medium heat, then add the meatballs in batches to avoid crowding the pan. Cook, turning continuously, until the meatballs are browned and cooked through, 3 to 4 minutes. Transfer the meatballs to a plate and cover with foil to keep warm while making the sauce.

Without wiping the pan, add the mushrooms and fry over medium–high heat until slightly browned and fragrant, a few minutes. Salt and pepper the mushrooms and sprinkle with the angelica seeds. Let them cook for 1 more minute, then sprinkle with flour and add the butter. Let them cook until the butter has melted. Add the heavy cream and rhubarb compote, stirring continuously until the sauce is thick and homogeneous, a couple of minutes. Add the meatballs back to the pan and stir to combine and reheat.

Serve piping hot with a side of mashed potatoes.

LAMB LIVER

WITH DULSE "BACON"

The key to a tasty liver is to not overcook it. The more you cook the liver, the more you will taste iron. Many people dislike the texture of liver and therefore I added some crunch in the form of seaweed. Dulse is harvested by hand in Iceland and is available both online and in health food stores. It is super salty so be careful when salting other elements of this dish.

YIELD: 4 SERVINGS

LIVER

1 lb (450 g) lamb liver

Garlic powder

Black pepper

1½ tbsp (20 g) butter

SIDES

1 tbsp (15 g) butter

1 red onion, cut into wedges

2 parsnips, shaved into strips

Salt and pepper

Several drops lemon juice

DULSE

Handful of dulse (dried leaves, not flakes)

Olive oil

Preheat the oven to 350°F (175°C). Line a baking sheet with parchment paper.

Cut the liver into 1-inch (2.5-cm) slices and season each slice with garlic powder and black pepper. Fry in butter for 2 minutes on each side (I like to use my grill pan) over medium-high heat. Remove from the pan, sprinkle with a little bit of salt and let rest for couple of minutes before serving.

In another pan, melt some more butter and sauté the onion wedges and parsnips until onions are tender and the parsnip strips are crisp, approximately 5 minutes. Add salt and pepper to taste and give the veggies a squeeze of lemon as well.

Place the dulse in a single layer on parchment paper, drizzle with olive oil and bake for 8 to 10 minutes until crispy.

Serve with potatoes, Ramps Pesto (page 140) or Pickled Beets (page 136).

LEG OF LAMB

WITH ROSEMARY, GARLIC AND BERRY MARINADE

I have probably eaten and cooked a gazillion legs of lamb in my lifetime. It is *the* go-to Sunday roast in Iceland and every family has their own methods and recipes for preparing this dish.

When I was growing up, my mom usually used garlic and heavy amounts of black pepper, but I am sharing with you my marinade of sour berries and lemon, which adds freshness and summery vibes to the meal. You can easily replace the currants with other sour berries, such as cranberries or gooseberries.

YIELD: 5 SERVINGS

4 lbs (2 kg) leg of lamb

1 tsp sugar

½ cup (75 g) red currants

1 clove garlic, minced

2 tbsp rosemary, minced

½ lemon, juice and zest

2 tsp salt

1½ tsp black pepper

Preheat the oven to 450°F (230°C).

Cut away any large chunks of fat, membrane and tendons from the leg of lamb, then pat it dry.

Sprinkle the sugar over the berries and let them sit for a couple of minutes before crushing them with a fork. Add the garlic, rosemary, lemon juice and zest, salt and pepper. Stir together then rub on the meat, making sure to cover every inch. Let the lamb marinate at room temperature for 45 minutes or in the refrigerator for up to 8 hours.

Place the lamb on an oven rack in a baking pan. Add 1 cup (240 ml) of water to the pan. Make sure the rack is high enough that the lamb is not sitting in the cooking water. Cook for 10 minutes, then turn the heat down to 350°F (175°C) and let roast for 70 to 80 more minutes, or until the lamb's internal temperature has reached 145°F (63°C) for medium rare or 155°F (68°C) for medium.

Let the meat rest for 15 minutes before slicing it. Make a jus from the collected juices by reducing them to half in a small saucepan and if you would like, add a little heavy cream to it right before serving.

Serve with Sugar-Glazed Potatoes (page 70) and a green salad.

LAMB CHOPS

WITH LOVAGE AND RAMPS

If you're like me and love to eat with your hands, then choose rib chops; but if you prefer a knife and fork, go for leg cutlets. Make sure not to buy lamb chops that have been frenched (see Note, page 65), simply because there is a lot of meat on the chops and when grilling each chop individually the fat gets crisp and caramelized. That would be a shame to miss out on!

YIELD: 2 SERVINGS

8 lamb chops

Salt and pepper

1–2 tbsp olive oil, divided

16 ramps

2 handfuls lovage

½ green apple

1 clove garlic

¼ tsp chili flakes

Salt and pepper the chops generously then throw them on the grill on medium-high heat for 3 minutes on each side. Drizzle olive oil and some salt onto the ramps and grill for 1 to 2 minutes until they are soft and slightly charred.

Pulse the lovage, apple, garlic and chili flakes in a food processor until coarse, slowly add the olive oil until you have a thick chimichurri-like sauce. Add salt and pepper to taste.

Serve the chops with the ramps on the side and a generous drizzle of the sauce.

RACK OF LAMB

WITH SEAWEED AND ALMOND CRUST

Don't be scared of the pairing of seaweed and meat, it sounds weirder than it tastes. Seaweed is naturally salty and therefore excellent for adding saltiness and an umami oomph to both meat and fish.

YIELD: 2 SERVINGS

1 rack of lamb (8 chops)

Black pepper

2 tbsp (30 g) butter

2 handfuls almonds

½ tsp angelica seeds (or fennel seeds)

¾ tsp arctic thyme (or regular dried thyme)

1 tbsp dulse

Pinch of salt

Olive oil

Preheat the oven to 375°F (190°C).

Trim the meat of all but a thin layer of fat, then French the rib bones halfway down (see Note). I do not recommend Frenching all the way down because the meat will automatically pull back a little and you will miss out on some delicious meat.

Crack some black pepper over the meat, then sear it in the butter in a pan over medium-high heat.

Pulse the almonds in a food processor until you have about ⅓ cup of rough almond meal. Grind the angelica seeds, thyme and dulse in a mortar, then mix with the almonds and a tiny pinch of salt.

Rub a little bit of olive oil over the meat and press the crumbs tightly onto it. Place the rack, with the fatty side up, in a roasting pan.

Roast for 25 minutes or until the center temperature reaches 125°F (52°C) for medium rare. Remove from the oven and let the lamb sit for 10 to 15 minutes before carving; the interior temperature will rise to approximately 130 to 132°F (54 to 56°C), which is perfect for a rosy middle.

Serve with roasted root vegetables and a crisp green salad.

NOTE: Frenched means a rack with the bones exposed. You can ask your butcher to do this for you or you can run a sharp knife along the fatty side and in between the bones and then scrape the meat off.

ROCK PTARMIGAN

WITH VANILLA

Rock ptarmigan is a small arctic bird that many Icelandic families eat for Christmas. The meat is very dark, quite dense in texture and has a very distinctive and strong gamey flavor.

It is hard to get your hands on a ptarmigan in other parts of the world, so I recommend you try this recipe with a quail or a small duck instead. Ptarmigans are very small, so I recommend one bird per person.

YIELD: 2 SERVINGS

2 rock ptarmigans, skinned

¾ stick (85 g) butter, room temperature

1½ vanilla beans

2 tsp (25 g) sugar

2 tsp arctic thyme (or regular thyme)

2 tsp salt

1 tsp black pepper

½ red onion

Several prunes, chopped

Preheat the oven to 350°F (175°C).

Rub the birds with butter.

Scrape the seeds out of the vanilla beans and mix them with the sugar using the flat side of a knife. Stir the vanilla, sugar, thyme, salt and black pepper together and sprinkle over the buttered birds.

Cut the onion in small chunks and place in the cavities of the birds, along with the prunes and empty vanilla pods.

Truss the birds with kitchen twine and sear in butter in a pan over medium-high heat for a couple of minutes on all 4 sides.

Transfer the birds to a roasting pan and roast in for 15 to 20 minutes or until the meat feels firm and juices run clear.

Serve with Brussels Sprouts with Smoked Butter and Sage (page 93) and Red Cabbage and Apple Slaw with Walnuts and Pomegranate (page 105).

DANISH CRACKLING PORK

WITH SUGAR-GLAZED POTATOES

Merry Christmas is the only thing I have to say about this dish. It is as Danish as it gets, but is also popular in Iceland for the holidays. Here is a quick history lesson for you: Iceland was a territory of Denmark until World War II, so many Danish traditions and dishes made their way into Icelandic culture.

You can use pork neck, belly or loin for this roast, just make sure it is boneless with a thick rind to crackle.

YIELD: 6 SERVINGS

PORK

2 lbs (1 kg) boneless pork roast with rind

Coarse salt

8 cloves

4 bay leaves

Black pepper

Pork bouillion (optional)

Preheat the oven to 375°F (190°C).

Use a sharp knife to score across the pork fat. The grooves should be ⅛ inch (0.5 cm) apart and go all the way through the fat (without cutting the meat).

Rub the roast generously with salt; make sure to get salt between all the scorings. Place cloves and bay leaves in the grooves and crack a little bit of black pepper over the rind.

Place the roast on a rack in a baking pan. Add 2 cups (480 ml) of water to the pan. Make sure the roast is perfectly horizontal and leveled for even roasting; if it is not, place balls of aluminum foil under the end that needs lifting.

Roast for 45 minutes, then remove from the oven and carefully pour the liquid from the baking pan into a pot. You should have about 2 cups (480 ml). Continue roasting the meat for 15 to 25 more minutes, or until the center temperature has reached 150°F (66°C). If the fat isn't crackling, turn the oven up to 420°F (220°C) for the last 10 minutes.

Let the roast rest for 15 minutes before cutting it into slices.

While the roast is resting, skim most of the fat off the liquid you reserved from the roasting pan. Bring the liquid to a boil and let it reduce a little. Taste the sauce and season with salt and pepper; add a little pork bouillon if you feel like the jus needs some more umami. Whisk until it thickens, then add a little heavy cream to taste.

(continued)

DANISH CRACKLING PORK

WITH SUGAR-GLAZED POTATOES (CONTINUED)

POTATOES

1 lb (450 g) small potatoes

⅓ cup (65 g) sugar

2 tbsp (30 g) butter

Peel and boil the potatoes in a pot of water until al dente, drain and let cool in the refrigerator until 20 minutes before serving. Melt the sugar over medium heat in a pan; try not to stir while the sugar is melting. When the sugar has turned a lovely amber color, add the butter and stir until melted. Add the potatoes to the sugar, stir and toss to coat them on all sides with the caramel, about 10 minutes.

Serve with Red Cabbage and Apple Slaw with Walnuts and Pomegranate (page 105) or Spiced Red Cabbage (page 72).

NOTE: You can serve any leftover meat on Danish Rye Bread (page 155) with a spoonful of Spiced Red Cabbage (page 72).

DUCK BREAST

WITH CRISPY SKIN AND SPICED RED CABBAGE

There is both duck and spiced cabbage on every Danish holiday table, so this dish really gets me in a holiday kind of mood (even though I cook it year-round). It's a warm, hearty and comforting dish that will soothe the harshness of a gloomy day and brighten up your winter blues—especially if you enjoy a good glass of red along with it!

YIELD: 2 SERVINGS

DUCK

2 duck breasts, with skin

Salt and pepper

Preheat the oven to 350°F (175°C).

The key to a tasty duck breast is perfectly rendered fat and crispy skin, so here's how you do it:

Pat the duck completely dry. Score the skin (be careful not to cut into the meat), season with salt and pepper, then lay the breasts onto a cold cast-iron pan, skin side down. Cook over medium-low heat for about 10 to 12 minutes, or until the fat has completely rendered and the skin is crispy.

While the fat is rendering, keep skimming fat off the pan, keeping just a thin pool on the pan at all times. (You can use the excess fat for your cabbage!)

When the skin is crispy, turn the breast over for 1 minute and then remove from the heat until the cabbage is just about ready.

(continued)

DUCK BREAST

WITH CRISPY SKIN AND SPICED RED CABBAGE (CONTINUED)

CABBAGE

½ head red cabbage

2 tbsp (30 g) duck fat (or butter)

1 orange, peeled

4 oz (120 ml) apple cider vinegar

4 oz (120 ml) balsamic vinegar

6 oz (175 ml) blackcurrant cordial

Small cinnamon stick

5 cloves

2 tbsp (28 g) brown sugar

Salt and pepper

Finely slice the cabbage and sauté it in duck fat until soft and "collapsed." Dice the orange and add it to the cabbage, along with every drop of orange juice from your cutting board. Add both vinegars to the pan, along with the cordial, cinnamon stick, cloves and sugar. Stir well. Cover the pot and let simmer over low to medium–low heat for at least 1 hour. Stir occasionally. Salt and pepper to taste.

When the cabbage is almost done, place the duck back into the pan and put into the oven for 5 minutes or until central temperature reaches about 135°F (57°C) for medium rare. Let the duck rest for 5 minutes before serving.

If you, like me, like to make every day a holiday, serve the duck with Sugar-Glazed Potatoes (page 70).

NOTE: Make a double batch of the spiced cabbage. Store it in sterilized jars in a cool, dark place for up to 6 months.

VEAL CHOPS

WITH SUNCHOKE PURÉE

This is a wintery dish, full of comfort and warm flavors.

The tarragon used in this recipe is definitely more linked to the French kitchen than the Scandinavian one, but with its anise and liquorice tones it fits perfectly with the Nordic flavor profile.

YIELD: 2 SERVINGS

SUNCHOKE PURÉE

1 lb (450 g) sunchokes

2 tbsp (30 g) butter, room temperature

Salt and pepper

Pinch of nutmeg

CHOPS

2 veal chops

Salt and pepper

2 tbsp (30 g) butter

Several sprigs fresh tarragon

SALAD

Pea shoots

Olive oil

Lemon juice

Salt and pepper

Peel the sunchokes and boil them in lightly salted water until tender, about 10 minutes. Drain, then purée them with butter, using an immersion blender or a regular blender. For a smoother version, press the purée through a sieve. Season the purée with salt, pepper and little bit of nutmeg to taste.

Salt and pepper the chops and fry them in butter for approximately 4 minutes on each side over medium-high heat, or until they reach an internal temperature of 150°F (65°C). Place a few sprigs of tarragon in the pan and baste the meat with the herb butter while frying.

Dress the pea shoots to your liking with olive oil, lemon juice, salt and pepper.

Spread the purée on two plates, place the chops on top and serve the crisp salad on the side.

Pickled Beets (page 136) are an excellent addition to this dish!

PHEASANT

WITH QUINCE AND BACON

In my mind, pheasant hunters are royal types in fancy—but never practical—hats, high socks and knickers, walking in thick fog with expensive dogs by their side, but that is probably just me watching too many period movies.

Nevertheless, pheasant is absolutely delicious and if you are new to the game scene, the pheasant is the bird to try first. The meat is white and only has a slight taste of game.

I use quince in this recipe but if it is not available where you live, use a pear instead.

YIELD: 4 SERVINGS

2 pheasants

½ stick (55 g) butter, room temperature

Salt and pepper

1 quince, diced

10 dates, halved

4 juniper berries, crushed

5 slices bacon, divided

2 sprigs rosemary

Preheat the oven to 450°F (230°C).

Wash and pat dry the pheasants. Rub the skin generously with butter and season the birds with salt and pepper. Fill the cavities with the quince, dates, juniper berries and 3 bacon slices cut into small pieces. Don't fill the cavities completely—air needs to be able to circulate. If you have more stuffing than you need, place the remainder in the bottom of the roasting pan and place the pheasants on top. Place one rosemary stick in the cavity of each bird, then truss the birds with twine.

Place 1 slice of bacon, cut in half, on top of each bird's breast, then place in the oven. Roast for 15 minutes, then turn the heat down to 375°F (190°C) and roast for 45 more minutes, or until the center temperature has reached 145°F (63°C). Let the birds rest for 15 minutes before carving.

Pour a little water into the roasting pan and swirl around. Strain the liquid into a jug, and serve as jus with the birds.

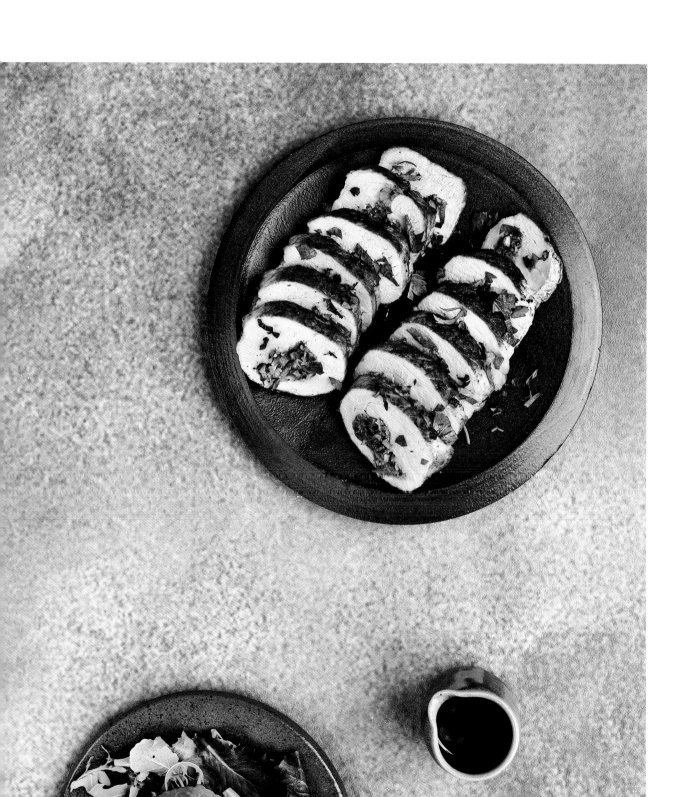

STUFFED PORK TENDERLOIN

WITH CELERY AND HAZELNUTS

This is a delicious family dinner, perfect for a Saturday night. It is best enjoyed with a glass of rosé or red.

YIELD: 4 SERVINGS

1 red onion, thinly sliced

3 tbsp (45 g) butter, divided

1 celery stalk, chopped

5 oz (140 g) celeriac, peeled and grated

¼ cup (30 g) hazelnuts, roughly chopped

½ tsp tarragon, dried

Salt and pepper

1 lb (450 g) pork tenderloin

Preheat the oven to 375°F (190°C).

Sauté the onion in a pan with 1 tablespoon (15 g) of butter over medium-low heat for about 7 minutes. Then add celery and celeriac along with another 1 tablespoon (15 g) of butter. Sauté for 10 minutes before adding the hazelnuts and tarragon, then sauté for 5 more minutes. Add salt and pepper to taste.

Meanwhile, butterfly the pork by cutting lengthwise along the tenderloin but without cutting through it. Open it up and cover with plastic wrap before pounding it flat. Remove the plastic wrap then place the vegetable stuffing evenly over the loin. Press the stuffing down firmly, then roll up the tenderloin tightly. Secure it with kitchen twine. Season the outside with salt and pepper.

Sear the meat in the remaining 1 tablespoon (15 g) of butter in an ovenproof pan, then place in the oven and roast for 15 to 20 minutes or until it reaches a central temperature of 145°F (63°C). Let rest for 15 minutes before cutting. Serve with a fresh salad and/or crispy fries.

NOTE: Marinated Dulse (page 139) goes great with this pork tenderloin.

WHOLE ROASTED GOOSE

WITH PRUNES, APPLES AND CINNAMON

Serving a whole bird is always beautiful—it looks elegant and sophisticated on the dining table and instantly adds a wow effect to your dinner party. This goose recipe is full of winter warmth and could easily be a holiday meal, or if you feel adventurous, could be served instead of the turkey on Thanksgiving.

In Iceland, we hunt pink-footed geese and greylag geese, but you can use any kind of goose you like for this recipe—no matter the name it will be delicious.

YIELD: 6 SERVINGS

1 whole goose (6–8 lbs [3–4 kg])

Salt and pepper

1 onion, roughly chopped

1 small apple, roughly chopped

10 prunes, roughly chopped

½ cup (75 g) red currants

1 cinnamon stick, broken

¼ cup (104 g) maple syrup

Preheat the oven to 425°F (220°C).

Clean the goose and pat it dry, trim off all excess fat and cut off the wing tips. Salt and pepper the goose, inside and out.

Mix the onion, apple, prunes, red currants and cinnamon stick then place in the cavity of the bird. Place on a rack in a roasting pan and roast for 20 minutes, then turn the heat down to 300°F (150°C) and roast for 3 hours, or until the bird has reached an internal temperature of 140 to 150°F (60 to 66°C).

About 10 minutes before the bird is ready, pour the maple syrup over it and return it to the oven.

Let the goose rest for 15 minutes before carving.

Serve with Roasted Beets with Liquorice (page 89), Preserved Pears (page 132) and giblet sauce if desired (see Note).

NOTE: If you have the giblets, you can use them to make sauce. Brown them in 2 tablespoons (30 g) of butter for 7 minutes on medium heat, then add a little water along with 2 roughly chopped carrots, 1 onion in wedges, a couple of roughly chopped celery stalks, 1 bay leaf and several sprigs of fresh thyme and boil for 45 to 60 minutes. Strain and mix with pan drippings after you remove the goose from the oven.

FROM THE GARDEN

SALADS SIDES

Living in the United States is so different from living in Iceland in terms of fresh vegetables and fruit. North America is so large and with multiple climates you can have almost everything, always. Things are always in season somewhere and you have easy access to everything you can think of. This is not the case in Iceland, where almost all fruit is imported and during winter very little other than root vegetables are available locally.

Iceland is not the country most known for indulging salads and greenery. Our meat- and fish-based cultural inheritance is still very present, but times are changing and with excellent import service the selection of fruit and vegetables is growing rapidly.

In this chapter, I tried to be true to produce grown in Scandinavia, even though, inevitably, a lemon or two found their way into the ingredient list.

FRIED CHIVE BLOSSOMS

I love chives! My grandma used to grow them in the darkest corner of her backyard and it was one of my chores to scoot out and cut a few stalks with scissors to sprinkle over salads and omelettes. I wish I could share this recipe with her, I know she would have enjoyed it. She was a big fan of deep-fried deliciousness.

These blossoms are a fun and delightful snack, perfect as amuse-bouche or as a part of a cheese plate.

YIELD: 20 BITE-SIZED PIECES

⅔ cup (80 g) flour

⅓ cup (40 g) cornstarch

⅔ cup (160 ml) seltzer

20 chive blossoms

Peanut oil

Salt

Whisk the flour, cornstarch and seltzer together into a light and fluffy tempura dough. Dip each blossom into the dough, then fry in 350°F (175°C) peanut oil for 20 to 60 seconds. Keep a close eye on them so they do not burn; if they burn they will taste bitter and unpleasant.

Sprinkle with salt and serve while hot and crisp.

BLISTERED RADISHES

WITH PICKLED RAMPS

Growing up I used to have a spot at a community garden where we grew pounds and pounds of radishes. I don't remember them ever being cooked, just served raw, as an afternoon snack.

Here they make a beautiful, warm spring salad that is both delicious and decorative. The tangy ramps pair excellently with the peppery radishes and it all comes together with the cottage cheese and freshness of the mint.

YIELD: 2-4 SERVINGS

1 lb (450 g) radishes

1 tbsp (15 g) butter

1 tbsp olive oil

Handful pickled ramps (or other pickled onions)

4 tbsp (55 g) cottage cheese

1 tsp lemon juice

Salt and pepper

Fresh mint, roughly chopped

Wash and trim the radishes; I keep most of them whole but if they are large I cut them in half.

Melt the butter and olive oil in a skillet and fry the radishes over medium heat until they blister and begin to brown, 5 to 7 minutes. Take the pan off the heat and add the pickled ramps and fresh mint.

Stir the cottage cheese and lemon juice together then toss with the radishes. Add salt and pepper to taste and sprinkle with some more fresh mint leaves.

ROASTED BEETS

WITH LIQUORICE

This pretty little dish makes an excellent appetizer or side dish. The sweetness of the beets and the tangy greens go beautifully together and the liquorice brings the whole dish together in a true Nordic way.

YIELD: 2 SERVINGS

1 bunch baby beets

Coarse salt

Liquorice powder

Several beet stems and greens

1 tbsp lime juice

½ tbsp white wine vinegar

Several drops honey

Edible herb blossoms: sage, chives and/or cilantro

Preheat the oven to 375°F (190°C).

Clean the beets with a brush but keep the skin on. Place each beet in foil, sprinkle with about ½ teaspoon of salt and about ¼ teaspoon of liquorice powder, close the foil tightly and place on a baking tray. Repeat for each beet. Roast in the oven for 30 minutes or until tender.

While the beets are roasting, crisp the stems and greens by placing them in an ice bath.

Whisk together the lime juice, vinegar, honey and a pinch of salt. Dress the leaves and stems in the dressing. Arrange the beets and greens on a plate and dust a little liquorice powder over. Sprinkle with salt and a few edible flowers.

BAKED LEEKS

WITH ROSEHIP AND TOASTED BARLEY

This is a lovely little dish with tangy, homemade rosehip vinegar drizzled over sweet, sweet leeks. Rosehips are all over Denmark, you can take a walk in any town or village and bushes will be filled with plump and brightly colored fruits. If you have access to fresh rosehip, by all means use them, otherwise stick to the dried buds described in the recipe.

You can make the vinegar 2 weeks in advance. I highly recommend you make a large batch and then use it for all your salad dressings—it's delicious! After the vinegar is made, this dish comes together in 30 minutes, but don't forget to plan accordingly.

YIELD: 2 SERVINGS

ROSEHIP VINEGAR

10 dried rosehip buds

½ cup (120 ml) distilled vinegar

¼ cup (60 ml) water

1 tsp brown sugar

Salt

LEEKS

2 leeks

Olive oil

Salt

BARLEY

¼ cup (40 g) barley

Black pepper

Preheat the oven to 350°F (175°C).

Start making the vinegar approximately 2 hours prior to serving time (or up to 2 weeks in advance). Bring rosehip buds, vinegar and water to a boil and let simmer for 7 minutes, then turn off the heat and crush the buds with a pestle or the back of a spoon. Put a lid on the pot and let steep for 30 minutes before adding the brown sugar and a pinch of salt. Bring to a boil again and let simmer for 5 minutes, then turn off the heat and let steep until the liquid cools to room temperature. Strain and discard solids.

For the leeks, trim both ends, then split them lengthwise and rinse in cold water. Let the water drip off before placing them in an ovensafe dish. Drizzle with olive oil and salt. Bake for 40 to 45 minutes, until they are softened and charred in spots.

Heat a frying pan to medium-high heat and toast the barley in a single layer on a dry pan while shaking the pan frequently to prevent the barley from burning. It will take about 5 minutes for the barley to crack and brown; it will have a nutty fragrance and flavor and an almost chewy texture.

Place leeks on a plate, and drizzle with rosehip vinegar, toasted barley and freshly ground pepper.

BRUSSELS SPROUTS

WITH SMOKED BUTTER AND SAGE

Brussels sprouts are one of my favorite vegetables. I serve them with everything and I could probably write a whole book about my love for them, but that will have to wait for another time.

I grew up eating Brussels sprouts sautéed in butter and sometimes caramelized in sugar. This version is a mixture of the two, with added smoke for some extra oomph.

YIELD: 2–4 SERVINGS

1 lb (450 g) Brussels sprouts

3 tbsp (45 g) Smoked Butter (page 119)

2 fresh sage leaves

½ tbsp maple syrup

Handful flat-leaved parsley

Wash the Brussels sprouts, remove the outer leaves and cut off the stem ends. Cut the Brussels sprouts in similar sizes; e.g., cut large ones in quarters, medium-sized ones in halves and keep the small ones whole. That way they will cook evenly.

Meanwhile, melt the butter in a pan over low heat, add the sage leaves and let cook with the lid on, for 5 minutes, then turn off the heat and let steep for 5 more minutes.

Turn up the heat to medium-high and when piping hot add the Brussels sprouts to the sage butter. Let them fry and char slightly, about 5 to 8 minutes, then turn the heat down to medium, add the maple syrup and cook for 1 to 2 minutes to gently glaze and caramelize the Brussels sprouts.

Right before serving, sprinkle finely chopped parsley over the pan.

NOTE: If you do not have smoked butter on hand, add a few drops of liquid smoke to salted butter instead.

CRUSHED POTATOES

WITH HORSERADISH AND DUCK FAT

Nearly every meal in Scandinavia is served with a side of boiled potatoes. They are inexpensive, easy to grow and taste so good when prepared in the right way. This is a great side dish for everything, be it simple fish or grilled meat.

You can, of course, make this dish without the duck fat for a vegetarian option, but if you don't mind the meatiness, please give the duck fat a chance, it is unbelievably delicious and transforms these potatoes from good to extraordinary.

YIELD: 2–4 SERVINGS

POTATOES

1 lb (450 g) potatoes

2 tbsp (30 g) duck fat

Salt and pepper

DRESSING

2 tbsp (30 g) fresh horseradish

4 tbsp (60 g) skyr

1 tsp lemon juice

½ tsp apple cider vinegar

Salt and pepper

TOPPINGS

Handful feta cheese

Handful flat-leaved parsley, finely chopped

Several celery leaves, finely chopped

Preheat the oven to 420°F (220°C).

Scrub the potatoes clean and boil them in lightly salted water for about 17 minutes, or until tender. Fish them out of the water, place in an ovensafe dish and crush them with a spatula until they crack. Drizzle generously with duck fat, salt and pepper. Roast in the oven for 25 to 30 minutes.

Peel and then grate the horseradish and stir together with the skyr and lemon juice, vinegar, salt and pepper to taste.

Spoon horseradish dressing over the piping-hot potatoes, crumble feta on top and decorate with the parsley and celery leaves.

FRESH POTATO SALAD

WITH APPLES AND SPROUTS

This is a creamy potato salad, but without the mayonnaise and with way less dressing than store-bought versions. On top of that, it packs lots of fresh elements to keep it crunchy and crisp and is perfect with grilled meat and fish!

YIELD: 2-4 SERVINGS

1 lb (450 g) small new potatoes

3 tbsp (40 g) natural sour cream (no stabilizer added)

1 tbsp olive oil

1 tsp Dijon mustard

1 tsp honey

Salt and pepper

1 green apple, cut into cubes

Radish sprouts

Chives, minced

Parsley, chopped

Peel the potatoes and cut them into similar-sized pieces and then boil them in lightly salted water until tender, about 10 to 20 minutes depending on the size. A good way to check if potatoes are cooked is to stick them with a fork; if the fork lets go right away the potatoes are ready, if it sticks they are not.

Stir together the sour cream, olive oil, mustard and honey, and salt and pepper to taste.

Toss the potatoes, apple and sprouts with the dressing. Garnish with chives and parsley.

GRILLED ASPARAGUS
WITH WILD EGG AND SEA TRUFFLE

You can use any kind of wild eggs in this recipe. If I am in Iceland in the spring, I like to use auk or great black-backed gull eggs, but goose, duck or quail eggs are all an option here.

Sea truffle is a seaweed harvested in Iceland; it is wonderfully salty and the truffly notes are not to be missed. You can buy sea truffle online and soon in some grocery stores in America.

YIELD: 2 SERVINGS

CROUTONS

2 slices rye bread, diced

1 tbsp olive oil

1 tsp garlic powder

Salt and pepper

ASPARAGUS AND EGGS

6 stalks asparagus

Olive oil

Salt and pepper

2 wild eggs

GARNISH

Sea truffle to taste

1 tsp angelica seeds, crushed

½ tsp smoked salt

Preheat the oven to 375°F (190°C).

Toss the bread with the olive oil, garlic powder, salt and pepper. Bake on a tray in the oven for 12 to 15 minutes, or until crisp and dry.

Drizzle the asparagus with olive oil, salt and pepper. Sear on a grill or piping hot grill pan for a few minutes. Meanwhile, fry the eggs in a little oil over medium heat.

Arrange the grilled asparagus, fried eggs and croutons on plates. Add the sea truffle, angelica seeds and smoked salt to taste.

SPICY KOHLRABI AND BEETS

This salad is a fun play with texture and flavor. It includes lots of surprises and your tastebuds will have a blast!

YIELD: 2 SERVINGS

5 oz (140 g) yellow beets, peeled and sliced paper thin

5 oz (140 g) kohlrabi, peeled and sliced paper thin

Juice from 1 lime

1 handful hazelnuts

Large bunch of watercress

Olive oil

Salt

5 oz (140 g) strawberries

Fresh chili, minced

Preheat the oven to 375°F (190°C).

Toss the beets and kohlrabi with the lime juice.

Roast the hazelnuts for 8 minutes in the oven. When cool enough to handle, rub them together between your hands or a clean kitchen towel to remove most of the skin and then roughly chop them.

Toss the watercress with a little olive oil and salt.

Keep a few of the strawberries whole; halve and quarter others.

Arrange everything on a big plate and sprinkle with chili.

SPRING SALAD

WITH RAMPS AND HERBS

This fresh, fragrant and flavorful salad will instantly kick-start your summer.

If you don't have cured egg yolks, use Parmesan cheese, and if ramps are not in season, use finely sliced leeks instead.

YIELD: 2 SERVINGS

1 bunch ramps

Handful sugar-snap peas

Handful lovage

Several sprigs tarragon

Several sprigs dill

Sage flower (or other edible herb flowers)

Salt

Olive oil

Cured Egg Yolk (page 115), grated

Cut the roots off the ramps and wash them, along with the peas and herbs. I like to cut a few of the snap peas lengthwise to open them up, but you don't have to. Toss the ramps, peas, herbs and flowers together. Sprinkle with salt and a few drops of olive oil and a generous amount of egg yolk.

Serve with fish or poultry.

RED CABBAGE AND APPLE SLAW

WITH WALNUTS AND POMEGRANATE

This is a simple slaw that goes with basically everything—meat or fish, in any season, rain or shine.

YIELD: 2-4 SERVINGS

1 tbsp olive oil

3 tsp sherry vinegar

2 tsp mustard

1½ tsp brown sugar

Salt and pepper

½ head red cabbage, shredded

1 green apple, shredded

½ pomegranate, seeded (see Note)

Handful walnuts, roughly chopped

Handful parsley, finely chopped

Whisk the olive oil, vinegar, mustard and brown sugar together until the sugar has dissolved; season with salt and pepper to taste. Toss the dressing with the cabbage, apple, pomegranate and walnuts and sprinkle parsley over the slaw.

NOTE: To remove the pomegranate seeds, hold the pomegranate, cut side down, in your hand and hammer the top with a wooden spoon. The seeds will fall right into your hand.

CHARRED GREEN CABBAGE
WITH RASPBERRY VINAIGRETTE

Cabbage is a hardy vegetable and grows well in cold climates. It is super versatile and can be prepared in a million different ways. Here, it is charred to make a beautiful and super-simple side dish for both meat and fish. You can char the cabbage until it is completly black and it will still taste delicious. The inside of the cabbage is sweet and tender and the charred bits give it personality and crunch.

YIELD: 4 SERVINGS

VINAIGRETTE

4 oz (115 g) raspberries

1 tsp sugar

1 tbsp sherry vinegar

1½ tbsp (25 ml) fresh orange juice

1 shallot, minced

CABBAGE

1 head green cabbage

Olive oil

Salt and pepper

Make the vinaigrette first so it can reach maximum flavor while you grill the cabbage. Wash and dry the raspberries, place in a small bowl and sprinkle with the sugar and let sit for couple of minutes before mashing them with a fork. Place in a cheesecloth and press the juices out into a clean bowl; you should be able to press all the juices out, only leaving seeds and dry pulp in the cloth. Stir the raspberry juice together with the vinegar, orange juice and shallot.

Cut the cabbage into wedges, drizzle generously with olive oil and season with salt and pepper.

Grill over high heat until tender and nicely charred on all sides, approximately 7 minutes per side.

Serve hot with raspberry vinaigrette drizzled on top.

FROM
THE PAST

CURED & SMOKED DELICACIES

Curing (dehydrating) and smoking are both ancient techniques to preserve food. In Iceland, which was once very isolated, people would hunt and fish and then cure and smoke their meat and fish to help them survive long, hard winters.

Today, even though the island is very well connected and everything the mind could dream of is imported, meat is still cured and smoked, not out of necessity but for pure pleasure and enjoyment.

In this chapter, I show you simple and easy ways to cure and smoke at home, where no fancy equipment or smoke chambers are required. My smoking setup includes a Dutch oven, aluminum foil, wood shavings, a steamer insert and a lid. It is that simple, but if you have a more professional setup, by all means use it!

CURED TROUT

WITH BEETROOT AND BIRCH

The beet in this recipe doesn't provide a whole lot of flavor due to the saltiness of the cured fish it is paired with, but it sure does add some drama with its red coloring and it looks absolutely beautiful.

This is a recipe for a small piece of wild fish. If you are making a whole side of a large trout or using farmed fish, adjust the recipe accordingly and keep in mind that curing time might be longer—up to 48 hours for very thick fillets. Check it regularly as it cures.

YIELD: 4 SERVINGS

1 tbsp (20 g) salt

1 tbsp sugar

2 tsp birch flakes

1 tsp black pepper

½ lb (225 g) wild trout fillet

½ beet, grated

Mix together the salt, sugar, birch flakes and black pepper. Place half of the spice mixture in a dish then place the trout fillet, skin side down, on top. Sprinkle the fish with the remaining spice mixture.

Sprinkle the raw beet on top of the fish. Cover the dish with plastic wrap and place in the refrigerator for 12 to 16 hours. If your fillet is very thick, you might have to add a little more salt and sugar and lengthen the curing time. The trout should be firm but not dry and should separate easily into thin slices. Wash any remaining salt and sugar off the cured fish, pat dry and store in the refrigerator until ready to serve.

Serve thin slices on sourdough bread with sour cream and radish sprouts.

GRAFLAX (CURED SALMON)
WITH MUSTARD SAUCE

If you go to a family gathering in Iceland there will be a buffet of large cakes, and in between marvellous meringues you will find toast with graflax and mustard sauce.

This is a recipe for a small piece of wild fish. If you are making a whole side of salmon or using farmed fish adjust the recipe accordingly and keep in mind that the curing time might be longer.

Serve the graflax as a part of your smorgasborg or as an appetizer, as it often was in my household at dinner parties in the 1980s.

YIELD: 6 SERVINGS

GRAFLAX

2 tbsp (35 g) coarse salt

2 tbsp (25 g) sugar

½ tsp mustard seeds

¼ tsp dill seeds

12 oz (340 g) wild salmon

2 tbsp fresh dill, finely chopped

SAUCE

¼ cup (60 g) Dijon mustard

¼ cup (60 ml) apple cider vinegar

2 tbsp honey

1 tbsp brown sugar

¼ cup (60 g) natural sour cream (no stabilizer added)

2 tbsp fresh dill, chopped

Salt and pepper

Mix together the salt, sugar and mustard and dill seeds. Place half of the spice mixture in a dish then place the salmon fillet, skin side down, on top. Sprinkle the fish with the remaining spice mixture along with the fresh dill. Cover the dish with plastic wrap and place in the refrigerator for 12 to 16 hours. If your fillet is very thick you might have to add a little salt and sugar and lengthen the curing time. The salmon should be firm but not dry and should separate easily into thin slices.

After curing, wash all remaining salt and sugar off the fish, pat dry and store in the refrigerator until ready to serve.

Whisk together the mustard, vinegar, honey and brown sugar until the sugar has dissolved. Then add the sour cream and dill, and salt and pepper to taste.

Serve the graflax on a toasted slice of sourdough bread with a dollop of sauce.

CURED EGG YOLKS

TWO WAYS

Curing egg yolks isn't particularly Nordic, but the technique is, so I will let it slide. Cured egg yolks are perfect for adding creaminess to both salads and pasta dishes.

You can make two types of cured yolks, one runny and the other firm. One is quick to make and the other takes some time, but both are delicious. The firm egg yolk can be grated as a salad topping and on avocado toast; the runny one is perfect for your Sunday brunch.

YIELD: 2 CURED YOLKS

3 oz (85 g) salt

3 oz (85 g) sugar

2 egg yolks

Stir the salt and sugar together and place half of the mixture in the bottom of a glass container. Form small dents with a back of a spoon and carefully place the egg yolks in the dents. Cover with the remaining salt and sugar. Cover the container.

For the runny egg yolk, let it cure for 1½ hours at room temperature before carefully brushing off the salt and sugar. Remove the yolk and slowly rinse the salt and sugar off in a bowl filled with cold water. Serve immediately on toast and top with chives and black pepper.

For the firm egg yolk, let it cure in the refrigerator for 5 days. Use a pastry brush to carefully brush off the salt and sugar after the 5 days of curing; the yolks should be firm but not completely dried out. For the last step, you can wrap individual yolks in a cheesecloth and let hang to dry in the refrigerator for 1 week or you can place them on parchment paper and bake at 150 to 175°F (66 to 79°C) for 1 hour.

Store the firm egg yolks in an airtight container in the refrigerator.

CURED GOOSE BREAST

WITH BLUEBERRY DRESSING

This is a delicious appetizer to serve your guests family style. The goose breast is gamey in the exact right way and together with the sweet blueberries it is the perfect fall and winter treat.

YIELD: 4 SERVINGS

GOOSE

5 tbsp (50 g) sugar

1 cup (250 g) coarse salt

2 goose breasts

1 tbsp rose pepper

1 tbsp dried rosemary

1 tbsp dried thyme

1 tbsp dried basil

1 tbsp dried tarragon

1 tbsp mustard seeds

1 tbsp dill seeds

BLUEBERRY DRESSING

¾ cup (195 g) Blueberry Jam (page 131)

2 tbsp balsamic vinegar

¾ cup (180 ml) olive oil

2 tbsp (30 ml) port

½ tsp black pepper

Several handfuls arugula

Mix the sugar and salt and cover the goose breast. Let sit in a closed container at room temperature for 5 hours then wash the breasts in cold, running water and pat them dry.

Stir the rose pepper, rosemary, thyme, basil, tarragon, mustard and dill seeds together in a container large enough to store the meat. Cover the breasts in the dry spice mixture and store in a closed container in the refrigerator for 3 days. Shake the container once every day to make sure the meat is covered with the spices.

For the dressing, whisk together the jam, vinegar, olive oil, port and black pepper.

Take the goose out of the refrigerator at least 1 hour before serving and thinly slice the meat.

Arrange arugula on a big plate, place goose slices on top and drizzle with the blueberry dressing.

SMOKED BUTTER

Smoked butter is such a simple way to add smoke to your dishes without having to smoke large pieces of meat or fish. Rub smoked butter over a whole chicken before roasting, melt and use as sauce for fish or whip it up with herbs and a little sour cream to serve with a home-baked sourdough loaf.

YIELD: 1 STICK

Birch and maple wood shavings

1 stick (115 g) salted butter

Sprinkle wood shavings over the bottom of a Dutch oven, then place a rack or steaming insert approximately 2 to 4 inches (5 to 10 cm) above the wood. (Because my rack doesn't have "feet" I rest mine on three balls made of aluminum foil.) Put a lid on the Dutch oven and place the pot on the burner of the stove and turn the stove on to medium heat. When you can smell the smoke, after 5 minutes or so, turn the heat down to medium-low.

Put the butter in a bowl (it will melt) and place it on the rack or insert in the smoker. Cover the pot with the lid but keep it open a tiny crack so that the smoke won't choke the butter completely and turn it bitter.

Let the butter smoke for 10 minutes. Taste the butter before removing it from the smoker and if you are satisfied with the flavor, skim off the solids and let the butter cool down and harden before using it. If you feel your butter can take a little more smoke, give it 5 more minutes before tasting again.

SMOKED SKYR

Heating low-fat cultured milk products is tricky as they tend to curdle, so for smooth smoked skyr you need to keep the heat super low. As with smoked butter, smoked skyr is a simple way to add smoke to your dishes without having to smoke large pieces of meat or fish. Use it for dressings or as a dipping sauce. It is absolutely essential with my Lobster Roll with Fennel Slaw (page 23).

YIELD: ½ CUP (125 G)

Birch and maple wood shavings

½ cup (125 g) skyr

Sprinkle wood shavings over the bottom of a Dutch oven, then place a rack or steaming insert approximately 2 to 4 inches (5 to 10 cm) above the wood. Because my rack doesn't have "feet" and it is not as wide as my pot, I rest it on three balls made of aluminum foil.

Put the skyr in a bowl and place it on the rack or insert in the cold smoker. Put the Dutch oven on a burner on the stove and turn the heat on medium for 3 minutes then turn it down to low and let the skyr smoke for 7 or 8 minutes covered with a lid. Leave the lid cracked slightly to allow the smoke to circulate so it does not turn the skyr bitter.

SMOKED ALMONDS

Smoked almonds are probably the best snack ever! They are great with beer and sour cocktails, and a lovely addition to a cheese plate or salads.

YIELD: 1 CUP (138 G)

1 cup (145 g) almonds

Sea salt

Sawdust (I like a mix of maple and birch)

1 tsp (or more) fresh rosemary, finely chopped

Soak the almonds in 2 cups (480 ml) of water for 30 minutes, then drain, pat dry and sprinkle with salt.

Put a thin layer of sawdust on the bottom of a cast-iron pan or Dutch oven, then place a rack or steaming insert approximately 2 to 4 inches (5 to 10 cm) above the sawdust. Put the lid on the pan and place it on a stove burner. Turn on the heat to medium and let the sawdust warm up; it will take about 5 to 7 minutes before it starts to smoke. As soon as you can smell the smoke, turn the heat down to medium-low and place the almonds in a single layer on the rack or insert (use aluminum foil over the rack or insert if the holes are too wide). Cover the pan again, but leave the lid open a crack so that the almonds don't turn bitter from too much smoke.

Smoke for 20 minutes, then sprinkle finely chopped rosemary over the almonds and smoke for 5 more minutes. Remove the almonds from the smoker and lay flat on parchment paper to harden. Sprinkle with some more salt and even some more rosemary if you are feeling adventurous.

SMOKED RED CURRANTS

Red currants are so beautiful and even though their tanginess can be harsh they are fun to cook with and absolutely excellent for jelly and jam making. A red currant jelly can transform gravy from dull to superb so I recommend you stock up and fill your freezer with these little red stars.

Smoked berries are not really common but they give a surprising burst to desserts, fish and meats, and using them for vinaigrettes is also lovely. If you cannot find red currants try wineberries, gooseberries or lingonberries.

Birch and maple wood shavings

Red currants

Sugar

Sprinkle wood shavings over the bottom of a Dutch oven. Place an aluminum foil-covered rack on top of the shavings. Spread the berries in a single layer on the foil. Cover with the lid but leave the lid open a crack so the smoke can circulate.

Put the Dutch oven on a stove burner and turn the stove to medium heat. When you can smell the smoke, after 5 minutes or so, turn the heat down to low and let the berries smoke for 7 minutes. Lift the lid and sprinkle a little bit of sugar over the berries. Put the lid back on and let smoke for 3 more minutes.

Remove the berries carefully because the sugar and heat will have softened them a little. Let them rest and cool down on a plate before using them.

If you are using berries other than red currants you might have to lengthen the smoke time. Keep an eye on them and taste during the smoking process; continue smoking until the taste is to your liking.

SMOKED MACKEREL

Mackerel is a strong-flavored and fatty fish, which makes it excellent for smoking. It is a super-tasty treat—great for a Nordic lunch buffet or as an appetizer at night.

Serve smoked mackerel with something pickled or spicy like horseradish, and adding some black pepper is a must. And needless to say, smoked fish is best friends with Danish Rye Bread (page 155) so you might want to bake a loaf or two as well!

YIELD: 1 SERVING

1 Boston mackerel

Coarse salt

Olive oil

1 sprig rosemary

Applewood chips

Gut and clean the mackerel. Pat it completely dry then cover it in salt and let it cure on a plate for 45 minutes on the kitchen counter. Then wash the salt off, dry completely, rub with a little olive oil and place the rosemary sprig in the cavity of the fish.

Cover the bottom of a cast-iron Dutch oven with aluminum foil, then add a small handful of wood chips on top of the foil. Place a rack or steaming insert approximately 2 to 4 inches (5 to 10 cm) above the wood chips.

Put the lid on the pot and place on the stove burner. Turn the heat to medium and let the chips warm up; it will take a few minutes before the chips start to smoke. As soon as you can smell the smoke, turn the heat down to medium-low and place the mackerel on the rack and smoke for 30 to 35 minutes. Leave the lid open a crack so that the smoke can circulate; otherwise your fish will turn bitter and unpleasant.

Serve smoked mackerel, hot or cold, on Danish rye with Dijon mustard, poached egg and chives.

FROM THE PANTRY

PICKLES, PRESERVES & PATÉS

When you start pickling and preserving it almost becomes addictive, especially when you grow your own produce. I truly enjoy my fall evenings in the kitchen, listening to jazz and testing jam recipes and experimenting with pickling every single thing I grow in my backyard.

Pickling and preserving doesn't only mean vegetables and fruits in Iceland. For example, a popular side for rice pudding with cinnamon is whey-pickled liver and blood sausage. But, in this chapter I am keeping it simple and you will find bulletproof classics such as Blueberry Jam with Birch (page 131), Pickled Beets (page 136) and Liver Paté (page 144), which no true Scandi can live without, mixed in with surprising delights like Ramps Pesto (page 140) and Marinated Dulse (page 139).

BLUEBERRY JAM
WITH BIRCH

This earthy and sweet jam is absolutely perfect with cheese of any kind and let's not even mention how spectacular it is with both lamb chops and on top of my Sourdough Loaf in Dutch Oven (page 151). I prefer to use wild blueberries but regular, store-bought berries are perfectly fine as well.

YIELD: ¾ CUP (200 G)

⅓ cup (65 g) sugar

½ cup (120 ml) water

2 tsp dried birch leaves

½ lb (225 g) blueberries

1 tsp pectin

Bring the sugar and water to a boil in a small saucepan, add the birch and stir until the sugar has dissolved. Remove from the heat and let steep for 30 minutes. Drain and discard the solids, reserving the syrup.

Add the blueberries to the birch syrup and bring to a boil. Lower the heat to low and let simmer for 5 minutes. Add the pectin, increase the heat to medium and let boil for 2 minutes before pouring into a sterilized jar. An unopened jar of jam will keep for several months in a dark and cool place. Refrigerate after opening.

PRESERVED PEARS

During winter I serve these pears with absolutely everything. They bring warmth to salty cheese and gamey meat and they will, without a doubt, amp up your morning porridge by a million. These pears have it all—they are sweet, spiced and slightly tangy from the vinegar and I highly recommend making a large batch. You will love them. I promise!

YIELD: 6 SERVINGS

2 lbs (1 kg) pears (Bartlett, Bosc, Anjou or Comice)

3½ cups (850 ml) water

¾ cup (180 ml) apple cider vinegar

1½ cups (330 g) brown sugar

4 star anise

1 (3-inch [8-cm]) cinnamon stick, broken into two

15 whole cloves

5 juniper berries

Peel the pears, leaving the stems on. Halve some of the pears and leave some whole (mainly because I think it looks pretty to have both).

Bring the water, vinegar and brown sugar to a boil along with the star anise, cinnamon stick, cloves and juniper berries. When the sugar has dissolved completely, lower the heat and, with the syrup simmering, slowly drop the pears in and let cook for 15 minutes or until tender but not mushy.

You might have to simmer the pears in batches, depending on the size of your pot. You need to be able to turn the pears and baste them while simmering so that they cook evenly.

When tender, fish the pears out of the syrup and place in clean, sterilized jar(s). Pour hot syrup and spices over the pears and screw the lid(s) on tightly. Let sit in a dark place for 2 to 4 weeks or up to 3 months before enjoying with cheese, meat or porridge. The pears will keep for several days in the refrigerator after opening.

RHUBARB SYRUP
AND COMPOTE

Rhubarb is super easy to grow, and it is one of the first things you can harvest from your garden in the spring.

Rhubarb syrup and compote are not only pretty and pink, they are delicious and you can use the two for basically everything: in rhubarb cocktails and sodas, on your pancakes, in cakes, in smoothies or margaritas, on yogurt, in salads … you get the picture!

YIELD: 2 CUPS (½ L)
SYRUP AND 1 CUP
(250 ML) OF COMPOTE

1 lb (450 g) rhubarb

6 tbsp (75 g) sugar

1 cup (120 ml) water

Seeds from ½ vanilla bean

Pinch of salt

Several mint leaves, chopped

2 strips lemon zest

Roughly chop the rhubarb into 1-inch (2.5-cm) pieces and place in a saucepan along with the sugar and water over medium heat. Let simmer until the rhubarb has softened and the sugar has completely dissolved, 5 to 10 minutes. Then drain the liquid into a clean pan and set aside while making the compote out of the mushy rhubarb jam you have left in your strainer or sieve. Add the vanilla and 2 tablespoons of the reserved liquid to the rhubarb "jam" and bring to a boil, stirring constantly so it doesn't burn. Salt to taste. Pour into a clean, sterilized jar. Store in the refrigerator for up to 4 weeks.

To make the syrup, add mint leaves and lemon zest strips to the reserved syrup. Bring to a boil and let simmer for a few minutes or until the syrup starts to thicken slightly. Turn off the heat and let it steep until the liquid is completely cold. Then strain one more time and discard the lemon and mint leaves. Pour the syrup into a clean and sterilized container and store in the refrigerator for up to 4 weeks, or in the freezer for up to 12 weeks.

PICKLED BEETS

Have you ever had liver paté with a pickled beet on top? Or a slice of smoked lamb with a side of these luscious and earthy gems? Well, if not, you need to pickle some beets as soon as possible!

The beets are easy to make but make sure you are wearing an apron; things tend to get a little messy and the beets will stain everything they touch.

YIELD: 20 SERVINGS

2 lbs (1 kg) beets (you can use any kind or color)

3½ cups (850 ml) distilled vinegar

5 oz (140 g) sugar

¼ tsp mustard seeds

¼ tsp dill seeds

8 cloves

12 black peppercorns

2 bay leaves

Boil the beets (with skin on) in lightly salted water until tender, approximately 30 to 40 minutes.

Place the boiled, hot beets in an ice bath and slip the skin off using your hands.

Meanwhile, bring the vinegar, sugar, mustard and dill seeds, cloves, peppercorns and bay leaves to a boil and let simmer until the sugar has dissolved, approximately 5 minutes.

Slice the peeled beets into thin slices (approximately ⅕ inch [5 mm]), place them into clean, sterilized jars and pour the vinegar mixture over. The beets are ready to consume in about 1 week, but you can store them in an unopened jar for 6 months in a dark, cool place. Refrigerate after opening.

MARINATED DULSE

(SEAWEED)

Ready for an umami explosion? This recipe isn't particularly Nordic, as I am using soy sauce and ginger, but dulse couldn't be more Icelandic, so even though I didn't grow up with marinated seaweed, it sure is a part of my everyday now and I serve it with everything from fish to pork chops. The longer it marinates the more the consistency becomes jam-like, which is perfect as a part of an indulgent cheese plate!

YIELD: 1 CUP (250 ML)

½ cup (120 ml) vinegar

½ cup (120 ml) water

¼ cup (60 ml) soy sauce

½ cup (110 g) brown sugar

1 garlic clove, grated

1 small piece of ginger, grated

1 oz (30 g) dulse (whole leaves, not flakes)

Bring the vinegar, water, soy sauce, brown sugar, garlic and ginger to a boil, then lower the heat to medium–low and let simmer until sugar has completely dissolved and the mixture is fragrant, approximately 5 minutes.

Pack the dry dulse into a sterilized jar, pour the pickling liquid over it and close the lid. Let marinate for 1 week before tasting. The longer it marinates the jammier and more flavorful it will become. Store opened jars in the refrigerator.

RAMPS PESTO

Ramps, the famous wild onions that make food lovers go wild, are in season only for a few weeks in the springtime. You will see people running around the forest hunting for the delicacy, and fights have broken out at farmers markets over the last bunch.

Ramps sure are delicious and there are endless ways of using them. Here is a pesto that I use as a smear for bread, on pasta, with roasted potatoes, as chicken marinade and the list goes on. I make a large batch and then freeze it in small portions. That way I can add ramps to my dishes way into the fall and if I stretch it, the last portion might reach the Thanksgiving table.

YIELD: 1½ CUPS (350 ML)

2 bunches (approximately 4 oz [115 g]) ramps

Handful almonds, roughly chopped

½ cup (40 g) grated Parmesan cheese

½ cup (120 ml) olive oil

Salt and pepper

Squeeze lemon juice

Wash and dry the ramps, then cut off the white bulb and purple stem. Use bulbs and stems for a vinaigrette, throw them in a stir fry or pickle them (see the recipe for Pickled Ramps on page 143).

Place the green ramp leaves, almonds and cheese in a food processor and pulse until everything is minced. With the processor running, pour the olive oil in and let spin for a few more seconds. Add salt, pepper and lemon juice to taste.

PICKLED RAMPS

These pickled ramps are ready to eat one week after pickling, but the longer they pickle the more flavorful they get, so it is up to your taste buds how long you keep them. I like mine the best after about 2 to 3 weeks in the refrigerator.

YIELD: TWO 2-CUP (½-L) MASON JARS

1 bunch ramps

½ tbsp salt

1 tsp black peppercorns

1 tsp mustard seeds

½ tsp dill seeds

½ tsp caraway seeds

1 bay leaf

1 cup (240 ml) water

1 cup (240 ml) distilled vinegar

1 cup (200 g) sugar

Clean the ramps and cut off the roots and green leaves. Use the greens for Ramps Pesto (page 140) or throw them in a Spring Salad with Ramps and Herbs (page 102).

Place the ramps, salt, peppercorns, mustard seeds, dill seeds, caraway seeds and bay leaf in a clean, sterilized, airtight jar.

Bring the water, vinegar and sugar to a boil, stirring until the sugar has completely dissolved, approximately 5 minutes. Pour the vinegar mixture over the ramps and spices and seal the lid tightly.

Let sit on your kitchen counter until it reaches room temperature, then place in the refrigerator for 1 to 3 weeks. An unopened jar will keep in the refrigerator for a few months. An opened jar will keep in the refrigerator for a couple of weeks.

LIVER PATÉ

Liver paté is a big part of the Nordic food culture and everyone I know got sent to school with a paté sandwich in their lunchbox multiple times a week.

You can use any kind of liver, but in Iceland, pork and lamb are the most common, whereas in Denmark, pork and veal are the most popular choices. In Iceland, paté is always eaten cold but in Denmark, it is a delicacy to serve it hot; I recommend you try both and see which you like best.

This is an easy version of a classic; I've jumped over a few steps to simplify it and quite frankly I can't taste a difference. This recipe makes a lot, so if you are not sure about your love for paté or if you are not expecting guests, cut it in half.

YIELD: 5 CUPS (1.25 L)

½ cup (120 ml) whole milk

1 bay leaf

½ tsp thyme

2 cloves

1 large yellow onion

2 tsp salt

½ tsp black pepper

1 lb (450 g) pork liver, ground

½ lb (225 g) pork fat, ground (unrendered)

1 egg

3 tbsp (25 g) flour

2 tbsp (30 ml) port

Several slices bacon

Start by infusing the milk by bringing it to the boil along with the bay leaf, thyme and cloves. As soon as it starts to bubble, turn off the heat and let steep with a lid on until it reaches room temperature. (I usually let it steep overnight.)

Preheat the oven to 350°F (175°C).

Pulse the onion along with salt and pepper in a food processor until very finely chopped, then add the liver and fat and pulse a few times. Add the infused milk, egg, flour and port and let the processor run until well mixed.

Divide the paté between ovenproof ramekins, small loaf pans or foil pans and place a piece of bacon or a bay leaf on top of each one. Then place the containers in a water bath (the water should cover half the pan) and bake for 35 to 45 minutes or until the central temperature has reached 165°F (75°C) and a toothpick inserted in the middle comes out clean.

I like to give my paté 2 minutes under the broiler before removing it from the oven; this gives it a nice caramelized and crusty surface.

Serve on Danish Rye Bread (page 155) with Pickled Beets (page 136).

NOTE: You can easily freeze the paté. Place it in a ramekin, cover with plastic wrap and store it unbaked in the freezer for up to 2 months. Bake it directly from the freezer, just add 15 minutes to the baking time.

FROM
THE
OVEN

SOURDOUGH & LOAVES

When I moved to the United States from Denmark, I found it impossible to find delicious, hearty bread, and that quickly became the thing I missed the most from home. So there was nothing else to do than start a sourdough mother and start baking.

I've been through multiple phases in my sourdough baking and my frustrations often hit the roof. But, the more you bake the more you get to know sourdough and the easier it becomes. You will learn to poke the dough and judge water levels without measuring. Practice makes perfect, so please, be patient.

SOURDOUGH STARTER

Making and keeping sourdough alive might look and sound like a lot of work but it truly isn't. It just takes a few minutes for a few days and after that it's literally seconds of your day to care for your sourdough. No biggie!

YIELD: 1 CUP (240 ML)

½ cup (60 g) whole-wheat flour, plus more for feeding

½ cup (60 g) all-purpose flour, plus more for feeding

¾ cup (180 ml) water

DAY 1: Stir the flours and water together in a nonmetal container. Leave the container uncovered on the kitchen counter for 2 days. Stir 2 to 3 times every day.

DAY 3: Pour one quarter of the sourdough out and feed it with 2 tablespoons of all-purpose flour, 2 tablespoons of whole-wheat flour and 3 tablespoons (45 ml) of water. You do not have to be precise with your measurements here; I usually add flour and water until I have the thickness I want. Return the "food" to the rest of the starter, then stir everything together well. Let it sit uncovered at room temperature.

DAY 5: Repeat the instructions for Day 3. Let it sit for a couple of days more until the mixture is bubbly and smells like beer.

DAY 7 (OR WHEN BUBBLY AND SOUR SMELLING): Repeat the instructions for Day 3. It will be ready to use in 8 hours.

(continued)

SOURDOUGH STARTER (CONTINUED)

Here are some tips for caring for and using your starter:

- When the starter is ready you can put a lid on the jar and keep it at room temperature.

- Stir your sourdough at least once every single day.

- Feed your sourdough three times a week. If you bake regularly this will happen automatically, but if you're not baking many loaves a week, repeat the instructions for Day 3.

- Don't forget to feed the sourdough every time you use some.

- Pour a little out and feed your sourdough 8 hours before you plan on using it.

- If you know you are not going to bake for a longer period, place the starter in the refrigerator until you are ready to start baking again.

- Keep your starter thicker during the summer months and thinner over the winter.

- The starter should smell more like beer than vinegar.

SOURDOUGH LOAF

IN DUTCH OVEN

Making delicious bread takes time, although not all of it is active time. You do need to plan ahead and start your loaf the day before you plan on serving it.

There are hundreds if not thousands of sourdough loaf recipes out there and tips and tricks on how to achieve the best results. A baker will tell you to measure everything in grams and check the temperature at every step, but I am not a baker so this recipe is how I make delicious bread with the least amount of effort in as little time as possible.

Here is my baking routine: I feed my sourdough starter early Friday morning, start making a dough at 6 p.m. Friday night, place my dough in the refrigerator at 10 p.m., take it out of the refrigerator at 6 a.m. and have a fragrant loaf at 9 a.m. for a Saturday breakfast.

YIELD: 1 LOAF

½ cup (120 ml) sourdough starter

1¼ cups (300 ml) water

3 cups (410 g) bread flour

2 tsp salt

Start by feeding your sourdough starter 8 to 12 hours before you plan on making the dough.

In a large bowl, mix together the sourdough starter and water, add the flour and stir the sticky dough with your hands or a wooden spoon until no streaks of flour are visible. Cover the bowl with a clean kitchen towel and let rest at room temperature for 30 minutes.

Pour the dough out on a clean surface, sprinkle the salt over it and knead by folding it, picking it up and folding it over itself again. Fold and stretch for about 7 minutes or until the dough starts to stiffen up. Put it back in the bowl and let rise for 1½ hours at room temperature. Fold the dough over itself a few times while still in the bowl, and let rise again for 1½ hours at room temperature. Fold the dough a few times before shaping the dough into a tight ball by tucking it under itself then spinning it on the table between your two flat hands.

Proof the loaf in a proofing basket or a bowl, in the refrigerator overnight (8 to 12 hours) or at room temperature for 4 hours if you are in a hurry.

(continued)

SOURDOUGH LOAF
IN DUTCH OVEN (CONTINUED)

Your loaf is ready to bake when you poke it gently and it keeps the dent for a while before it slowly comes back. If it springs right back the dough needs more proofing time, if the dent doesn't spring back the dough is over proofed.

Take the dough out of the refrigerator, let it "wake up" and come to room temperature, approximately 1 hour.

Preheat the oven to 480°F (250°C).

Place an empty Dutch oven with the lid on in the oven and leave it to heat up for 30 minutes. Take the hot Dutch oven out and carefully turn the dough ball into it. To help let the steam out while baking, score the dough with a sharp knife or a razor blade. Put the lid back on and bake for 30 minutes. Then turn the heat down to 450°F (230°C), take the lid off and bake for 15 more minutes.

NOTE: You can easily make two loaves at a time. Double the recipe then divide the dough in two right before placing it in the refrigerator.

DANISH RYE BREAD

If there weren't already a Prince of Denmark this bread would be it! This is *the* bread and almost the only bread. Everybody eats it, everybody loves it and you simply cannot get anything more Danish than this bread. Period.

Danish rye is eaten as an open sandwich (smørrebrød) or one slice folded in two (klap sammen). Believe me, there are rules on which toppings go together and which do not—I will never forget the look on my mother-in-law's face when she watched me put sausage and cheese on the same piece of bread. But you have my permission to do as you please, because this savory and hearty bread goes great with everything.

YIELD: 2 LOAVES

¾ cup (175 ml) sourdough starter

1½ cups (350 ml) water

17 oz (480 g) rye flour

3 tsp (18 g) salt

8 oz (225 g) cracked rye

4 oz (115 g) raw and shelled sunflower seeds

2 oz (55 g) pumpkin seeds

2 oz (55 g) flax seeds

2 tbsp barley malt syrup

Butter or oil for greasing

Feed your sourdough starter 8 to 12 hours before you start the baking process.

Whisk the sourdough starter with the water, flour and salt and stir until homogenous. Let proof at room temperature for 8 hours.

While the dough is proofing, soak the cracked rye and sunflower, pumpkin and flax seeds in water to soften them and leave at room temperature for 8 hours. Drain the kernels thoroughly and let drip. Add to the dough along with the barley malt syrup and knead with your hands (in the bowl) until incorporated.

Divide the dough between two greased loaf pans and let proof under plastic wrap for 2½ hours. The dough will rise a little bit. You will see small air bubbles on the surface when it is ready to bake.

Preheat your oven to 450°F (230°C).

Place the loaves in the preheated oven and bake for 10 minutes, then turn the heat down to 400°F (200°C). Let the bread bake for approximately 50 more minutes.

SOURDOUGH PIZZA

Well, Scandis can absolutely not take credit for inventing the pizza. But, I thought you might like a delicious sourdough pizza recipe. And if you top it with Brussels sprouts, beets and herbs we can call it a Nordic pizza, right?

YIELD: FOUR 10-INCH (25-CM) PIZZAS

⅓ cup (80 ml) sourdough starter

1½ cups (350 ml) water

3¾ cups (500 g) flour, tipo 00 (or bread flour)

1½ tsp (9 g) salt

2 yellow onions, thinly sliced

2 tbsp (30 g) butter

2 tbsp balsamic vinegar

1 tbsp sugar

Brussels sprouts, shredded

Sugar snap peas, whole or cut lengthwise

Fresh mozzarella, sliced

Fresh herbs of your choice (e.g., basil, mint, dill)

For this recipe you need to plan ahead, but it will be worth it. First, feed your sourdough starter 8 to 12 hours before making the dough. I usually feed my sourdough starter at 8 a.m. the day before I want to make pizza. I then start making the dough around 6 p.m. that same day and place the preproofed and folded dough in the refrigerator around 9 p.m. I form the dough at 9 a.m. the following morning and let proof at room temperature for 6 hours, then place in the refrigerator until ready to bake at 6 p.m.

Whisk the sourdough starter and water together then add flour and salt, and stir to form dough. Turn out the dough on a clean working surface and knead it by folding it over, picking it up and throwing it on the table with strong and confident hands for 10 minutes. Place the dough back in the bowl and let it proof under plastic wrap or a kitchen towel at room temperature for 3 hours. Every 30 minutes fold the dough over itself a few times. After 3 hours of proofing and six folding sessions, cover the bowl with plastic wrap and place it in the refrigerator for 10 to 12 hours.

Remove the dough from the refrigerator and bowl, divide into four even-sized pieces and form each piece into tight balls by spinning the dough on the counter between flat hands. Place the balls into a lightly greased baking dish, cover the dish with plastic wrap and let proof at room temperature for 6 hours. The dough should be relaxed and puffy. You can now bake your pizza or place dough in the refrigerator until ready to bake (up to 6 hours). Preheat the oven to 500°F (260°C). If you are using a pizza stone or steel, preheat it in the oven for 30 to 60 minutes before placing the pizza on top.

For the toppings, sautée the onions in butter with a pinch of salt over medium heat for 20 minutes, then add the vinegar and sugar. Let the vinegar evaporate and voilà, you have succulent sweet onions. With flour on your hands, form one pizza at a time (the dough will be sticky), top each with the toppings—Brussels sprouts, snap peas, onions and mozzarella—and bake for 8 minutes. Decorate the pizza with fresh herbs right before serving.

FROM THE HEART

SWEET TREATS & DESSERTS

Desserts make me oh so happy, a piece of cake or spoonful of ice cream can easily turn the blues into bliss at the first bite.

Berries, rhubarb, cream and cardamom. Summer treats and winter comforts. Old classics and new discoveries. From the bottom of my heart, thank you for reading along. Please, have some dessert!

ICELANDIC SKYR CAKE

The no-bake Icelandic Skyr Cake is always a big hit with its fresh and not-too-sweet flavor and both crunchy and soft texture. If you are a fan of cheesecake you will love this one. You can make skyr cake weeks in advance—just put it straight into the freezer after you make it.

You can use any flavored skyr you like; I prefer blueberry but vanilla is also delicious.

YIELD: 12 SERVINGS

8 oz (225 g) digestive biscuits with dark chocolate

1 stick (115 g) butter, melted

1 lb (450 g) blueberry skyr

2 eggs

Seeds from ½ vanilla bean

1 cup (250 ml) heavy cream

4 tbsp (60 ml) milk

2½ tbsp (25 g or 8 sheets) gelatin powder

Line a round, 8-inch (20-cm) springform pan with parchment paper. Crush the biscuits into a coarse meal and mix with melted butter. Press in the bottom of the pan and make an even layer. Place in the refrigerator while you mix the cake.

Whisk the skyr, eggs and vanilla together in a bowl. In a separate bowl, whip the cream until medium stiff peaks form. Fold the cream into the skyr mixture.

Heat the milk in a small saucepan over medium-low heat and add the gelatin. Stir well until the gelatin is dissolved. Pour into the skyr and cream mixture and fold to combine. Pour over the biscuit layer and cover the pan with plastic wrap. Let set in the refrigerator for at least 8 hours or freeze straightaway for a later use. If freezing the cake, thaw for 8 hours in the refrigerator or 3 hours at room temperature.

Decorate the cake with fresh berries and edible flowers.

RØMMEGRØT

WITH LAVENDER AND SMOKED CURRANTS

Rømmegrøt is a classic Norwegian pudding, but after reading this book you should know that I tend to make things my own way, and this recipe is no exception. I infused the pudding with lavender and added both sugar and smoked currants to this traditionally savory pudding. It might not be the real thing but it is definitely inspired by and related to the original, so I'm calling it Norwegian either way.

YIELD: 4 SERVINGS

PUDDING

1½ cups (350 ml) whole milk

10 lavender blossoms

3 tbsp (40 g) sugar

1 tsp pure vanilla extract

1 cup (30 g) natural sour cream (no stabilizer added and preferably not ultra-pasteurized)

⅓ cup (40 g) flour

Pinch of salt

TOPPINGS

1 tbsp (13 g) sugar

½ tsp cinnamon

¼ stick (30 g) butter, melted

Smoked Red Currants (page 124)

Warm the milk to the boiling point along with the lavender and sugar, then lower the heat to medium-low and let simmer until the sugar has dissolved, a few minutes. Remove from the heat, put a lid on the pan and let steep until the mixture comes to room temperature, approximately 2 hours. Strain, discard the lavender and stir in the vanilla.

Heat the sour cream in a pot over medium heat and while whisking constantly sprinkle the flour over, a little at a time. If the sour cream separates, skim off the solids and set aside. Continue stirring, adding flour and whisking until you have a thick dough-like substance. Add the infused milk, stirring constantly, until completely mixed. Raise the heat to medium-high and bring to a boil. Cook until the mixture is glossy and smooth, 5 to 7 minutes. Salt to taste.

Stir the sugar and cinnamon together for sprinkling. Melt the butter, or if you skimmed butter off the sour cream use that.

Divide the pudding into four bowls, drizzle with melted butter, place smoked berries on top and sprinkle with cinnamon sugar. The pudding can be served hot or cold.

NOTE: You can substitute unsmoked berries of any kind for the smoked red currants.

BLUEBERRY SOUP

Wild blueberries are ideal for this dessert, and in fact the Icelandic blueberries meant for this soup are not called blueberries, they are bilberries. However, you are probably not going to find those, so using blueberries is just fine.

YIELD: 4 SERVINGS

½ cup (100 g) sugar

¾ cup (180 ml) water

2 tsp (arctic) thyme

Zest from ¼ lemon

14 oz (400 g) blueberries

1 tsp balsamic vinegar

Pinch of salt

½ cup (120 ml) heavy cream

Seeds from ½ vanilla bean

Bring the sugar and water to a boil in a small saucepan, add the thyme and lemon zest. Stir until the sugar is completely dissolved. Remove from the heat and let steep for 30 minutes. Drain and discard the solids, returning the syrup to the saucepan.

Add the blueberries to the syrup and bring to a boil then lower the heat and let simmer over low heat for a few minutes or until the berries begin to burst. Mash the berries as much as you can and then strain the soup into a clean pot, discarding the solids.

Add the balsamic vinegar and salt to taste.

Whip the cream with the seeds from the vanilla bean until soft peaks form.

Ladle the soup into four bowls. Place a dollop of cream on each bowl. Serve the soup either hot or cold—it is delicious both ways.

APPLE PORRIDGE

WITH NORDIC DUKKAH

This is another recipe with something that isn't originally from Scandinavia that I have made Nordic with the ingredients chosen. Dukkah is an Egyptian spice and nut blend that comes in millions of combinations but traditionally contains coriander, cumin and caraway seeds.

Even with the nontraditional topping, the apple porridge in this recipe is totally Danish, I promise.

YIELD: 6 SERVINGS

APPLE PORRIDGE

2 lbs (1 kg) apples, peeled, cored and cut into 2-inch (5-cm) cubes

⅓ cup (60 g) sugar

½ cup (120 ml) water

1 vanilla bean

DUKKAH

¾ cup (120 g) almonds

2 tbsp angelica seeds

1 tsp dill seeds

1 tsp caraway seeds

1 tsp sugar

Place the apples, sugar and water in a saucepan. Scrape the seeds out of the vanilla bean and add to the apples. Bring to a boil then lower the heat to medium–low and let simmer for 30 minutes or until the apples are soft and mushy. Remove the vanilla bean.

I like my porridge with a few apple chunks but you can run an immersion blender through the porridge for a smoother version.

Toast the almonds in a dry pan over medium heat until they start to brown and become fragrant. Remove from the pan and place in a food processor or blender. Add the angelica seeds, dill seeds and caraway seeds to the pan and toast for a minute or two over medium heat, then add to the food processor along with the sugar. Pulse a few times or until the almonds are finely chopped and well mixed with the spices. If you want to stay true to the dukkah (which means to pound) you can use a mortar and pestle to make it.

Serve the apple porridge hot or cold with a heaping spoonful of dukkah and vanilla ice cream.

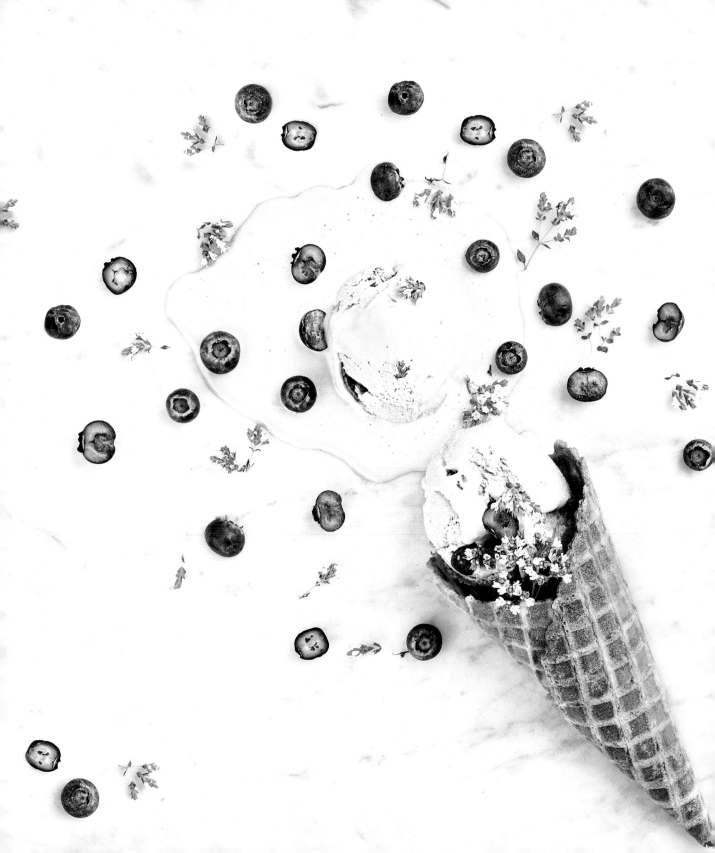

LIQUORICE ICE CREAM

Liquorice is probably the most-loved flavor for sweets throughout Scandinavia. Gummies, hard candy, filled chocolates and of course liquorice ice cream are found everywhere. After moving to the United States I found good liquorice hard to come by, so I make it myself by infusing different things with store-bought Danish liquorice powder.

You may be thinking that you hate black liquorice, but pretty please, give this ice cream a chance. I bet it will surprise you.

YIELD: 1 QUART (1 L)

6 egg yolks

¾ cup (150 g) sugar

2 cups (500 ml) 2% milk

3 tbsp liquorice powder

2 cups (500 ml) heavy cream, ice cold

Whisk the yolks and sugar until light and fluffy, about 6 minutes with electric whisker or electric mixer.

Heat the milk and liquorice powder in a saucepan over medium heat until almost boiling. Pour it into the egg-yolk mixture in a thin, steady and slow stream while whisking constantly. Return the mixture to the saucepan and bring to a boil, then lower the heat to medium and let simmer for 3 to 4 minutes, stirring constantly. The mixture will thicken but not become as thick as custard.

To stop the cooking quickly, pour the mixture into a bowl set in an ice bath, then add the ice-cold heavy cream and stir until the mixture is chilled to room temperature. Ladle into a jug and place in the refrigerator for 2 hours or overnight. Churn in an ice-cream maker.

NOTE: If you do not have an ice-cream maker, after adding the heavy cream, pour the mixture directly into a loaf pan. You can add a few drops of alcohol (e.g., vodka, rum or bourbon), which will keep the ice cream soft. Place in the freezer and whisk vigorously every 30 minutes for the next few hours while the ice cream is freezing.

CHOCOLATE AND CARAMEL TART

WITH SKYR

I finally found a way to make dulce de leche with skyr, and even though this is not your typical caramel tart, it is delicious with its slightly sour and not-too-sweet caramel.

YIELD: 12 SERVINGS

TART SHELL

1 stick (115 g) butter

3 tbsp (27 g) powdered sugar

1 egg yolk

½ tsp vanilla extract

1¼ cups (150 g) flour

3 tbsp cocoa

½ tsp salt

CARAMEL

3 cups (750 ml) whole milk

2 cups (500 g) unflavored skyr

1 cup (200 g) sugar

2 tsp baking soda

½ tsp salt

TOPPINGS

2 tbsp (20 g) white chocolate chips

Several drops coconut oil

Freeze-dried blueberries

Fresh blueberries

1 cup (250 ml) heavy cream

2 tbsp Kahlua (optional)

In a food processor, pulse the butter and powdered sugar until smooth, then add the egg yolk and vanilla extract and pulse a few more times. Add the flour, cocoa and salt and pulse until just incorporated. Press the dough evenly into an 8- to 9.5-inch (20- to 24-cm) pie pan (I use a tart pan with a loose bottom) then chill for 1 hour.

Preheat the oven to 375°F (190°C).

Prick the tart shell a few times with a fork. I highly recommend adding pie weights to keep the shell in place. Bake for 15 minutes. Let cool completely.

Whisk the milk, skyr, sugar and baking soda in a large pot. Bring to a boil while stirring constantly, then lower the heat to low and let simmer for 30 to 45 minutes, or until you have a smooth amber-colored caramel. While simmering the mixture it will foam, so use a large pot or divide it into two pots to make it easier to avoid having the caramel boil over. Don't let the foam scare you, just keep an eye on the caramel to make sure it doesn't burn. Stir and scrape the bottom of the pot every 3 to 5 minutes.

Add salt to the caramel before pouring it through a strainer and let cool to room temperature before pouring it into the prebaked tart shell. Chill in the refrigerator for at least 3 hours.

Melt the chocolate over a warm water bath or in a double boiler, then stir in a few drops of coconut oil. Using a fork or pastry brush drip a Jackson Pollack–inspired pattern of dribbles and drops on the tart. Decorate with crushed freeze dried berries and fresh blueberries.

Whip the cream with the Kahlua until soft peaks form; serve on the side.

BIRCH GRANITA

WITH PICKLED BLUEBERRIES AND RHUBARB FOAM

You know that fresh smell of the woods on a freezing-cold winter day? Did you ever want to transfer precisely that smell into a dessert? Well, I've done it for you and have created this Nordic flavor explosion. This is a simple and fresh dessert that could also be served as a palate cleanser between courses. Now breathe in and taste the North.

YIELD: 6 SERVINGS

GRANITA

2 cups (500 ml) water

⅓ cup (65 g) sugar

1 green apple, cubed

⅓ cup dried birch leaves

1 tbsp lemon juice

BLUEBERRIES

1 cup (250 ml) water

⅓ cup (80 ml) vinegar

2 tbsp (25 g) sugar

4 cloves

2 cardamom pods

1 cup (150 g) blueberries

RHUBARB FOAM

½ cup (120 ml) Rhubarb Syrup (page 135)

1 tsp soy lecithin

Bring the water, sugar, apple and birch leaves to a boil in a saucepan. Lower the heat to medium–low and let simmer until the sugar has dissolved and the apple is tender, 3 to 4 minutes. Turn off the heat and let the mixture steep with a lid on for 30 minutes.

Transfer the mixture to a blender, add the lemon juice and purée. Press through a sieve into a shallow baking dish and place the mixture in the freezer for 2 hours. After 2 hours, stir, break up and shave the granita with a fork every 30 minutes for the next 2 to 3 hours. When you have an icy crumble, pack it loosely in a closed container and store in the freezer until ready to serve.

Bring the water, vinegar, sugar, cloves and cardamom pods to a boil then lower the heat to medium–low and let simmer until the sugar has dissolved, 4 to 5 minutes. Place the blueberries in a mason jar or other airtight container and pour the warm liquid over them. Let stand on the kitchen counter until the mixture has reached room temperature, then place in the refrigerator. Let pickle in the refrigerator for 8 to 24 hours.

Pour the rhubarb syrup into a bowl, sprinkle with lecithin and use an immersion blender to whisk until foam forms. Tilt the bowl a little so that only two-thirds of the blender is immersed in the liquid, that way plenty of air gets in the mix to create the bubbles. The foam will stay firm for about 1 hour, so I recommend making it close to serving time.

Arrange the granita and pickled blueberries on plates and garnish generously with rhubarb foam.

THE GROWN-UP CAKE

WITH DATES AND HAZELNUTS

This cake was a part of the holiday baking traditions in my home when I was growing up, and for an unknown reason I used to call it the grown-up cake. Back then it was served with a super dark and very sweet rhubarb jam and whipped cream. My version is a little lighter; I still use both rhubarb and cream for the filling, just in a more fluffy and pinkish way.

YIELD: 12 SERVINGS

CAKE

1 cup (150 g) dates, roughly chopped

¼ cup (60 ml) water

2 eggs

½ cup (110 g) brown sugar

½ tsp vanilla extract

1½ cups (100 g) hazelnut flour

1 cup (85 g) unsweetened coconut flakes

1½ tsp baking powder

2 oz (60 g) dark chocolate, roughly chopped

½ tsp salt

CREAM

½ vanilla bean

3 tsp sugar

4 oz (115 g) strawberries, halved

6 oz (170 g) rhubarb, chopped into 1-inch (2.5-cm) pieces

1 cup (250 ml) heavy cream

Preheat the oven to 350°F (180°C). Grease and line an 8-inch (20-cm) round baking pan with parchment paper.

Put the dates and water in a saucepan, bring to a boil then lower the heat to medium–low and let simmer for 5 to 7 minutes or until the water has evaporated and the dates have softened slightly.

While the dates are simmering, cream the eggs and sugar for 5 minutes with an electric whisk or in a stand mixer, adding the vanilla at the end. In a separate bowl, stir together the hazelnut flour, coconut, baking powder, chocolate and salt.

Add softened dates to the flour mixture, stir to combine and then fold in the eggs.

Spread the dough evenly into the prepared pan. Bake for 35 minutes or until a toothpick inserted in the middle comes out clean.

Scrape the seeds out of the vanilla and mix together with the sugar. Place the strawberries and rhubarb in an ovenproof dish, sprinkle with the vanilla sugar, place the empty vanilla bean on top and bake for 30 minutes. Let cool completely, remove the vanilla pod and stir and mash the rhubarb and strawberries together.

Whip the cream until medium-hard peaks form then fold in the rhubarb/strawberry compote. Spread the cream/compote mixture on top of the cake and decorate with edible flowers, berries or rhubarb ribbons.

NOTE: Stock up on rhubarb in the springtime, cut it into 1-inch (2.5-cm) pieces and freeze in an airtight container. That way you can make summery desserts all year long.

FLØDEBOLLER

Chocolate covered, creamy, marshmallowy, airy deliciousness is what flødeboller are all about.

They are time-consuming and a bit messy to make, I will not lie. However, they are so absolutely worth it!

This is the basic recipe with vanilla filling and dark chocolate but there is plenty of room to experiment. May I suggest liquorice or raspberry filling with white chocolate?

YIELD: 20 PIECES

3 tbsp (45 ml) water

5 oz + 2 tbsp (165 g) sugar, divided

2.5 oz (75 ml) glucose

2 tsp lemon juice

1 tsp pure vanilla extract

4 egg whites

20 small waffle wafers (store bought or homemade)

8 oz (225 g) dark chocolate, divided

Shredded coconut, freeze-dried fruit or nuts for sprinkling

NOTE: If you want to be even more Danish, you should use marzipan for the bottom layer instead of wafers. Simply slice or cut out thin disks and bake at 350°F (175°C) for 7 minutes or until lightly browned. Let cool completely before piping on the merengue.

Bring the water, 5 ounces (140 g) of sugar, glucose and lemon juice to a boil in a small saucepan. Let the syrup boil until it reaches 242°F (117°C). Remove from the heat and set aside. Stir in the vanilla.

Whisk the egg whites and 2 tablespoons (25 g) of sugar with a stand mixer or electric whisk until soft peaks form, approximately 3 minutes. Pour the syrup mixture slowly, in a thin but steady stream, into the egg whites, while whisking constantly. Whisk or mix for 8 minutes or until the whites are completely stiff and you can turn the bowl upside down without them falling out.

Transfer the egg white mixture to a piping bag and pipe tall spirals onto the waffle wafers. Let the flødeboller stand in a cool place to dry for 6 hours (preferably longer or overnight).

When ready to assemble the flødeboller, slowly melt two-thirds of the chocolate over a warm-water bath or in the top of a double boiler and bring it to 113°F (45°C). Chop the remaining one-third of the chocolate and stir together with the melted chocolate; adding the chocolate should bring the temperature down to 82 to 84°F (28 to 29°C). Continue stirring and the chocolate should slowly heat up to 88 to 89°F (31 to 32°C), which is the perfect temperature for a shiny chocolate that will have a nice crack to it when you bite into it.

Place one flødebolle on an offset spatula and ladle the tempered chocolate over, let it drip before placing the flødebolle on a rack to harden. Add sprinkles (coconut, freeze-dried fruit or nuts) while the chocolate is still wet.

Store the flødeboller in a dark and cold place. I keep mine in the refrigerator because I love, love, love cold chocolate, but that is not necessary.

KOLDSKÅL AND KAMMERJUNKER

Koldskål is a true Danish summer classic. It is a refreshing, cold, custardy buttermilk soup with vanilla and lemon. And let's not forget the yummy biscuits that go on top—kammerjunker—which may or may not be totally addictive! I am absolutely confident when I say that this will become your go-to summer dessert from now on. Seriously, it is delicious!

YIELD: 1 QUART (1 L)

KOLDSKÅL

3 large egg yolks

4 tbsp (50 g) sugar

1 vanilla bean

2 cups (500 ml) buttermilk

2 cups (500 ml) plain yogurt (full fat)

Juice and zest from ½ lemon

KAMMERJUNKER

2 cups (250 g) flour

1 tsp baking powder

4 tbsp (50 g) sugar

Seeds from ½ vanilla bean

Zest from ¼ lemon

Pinch ground cardamom

1 egg

4 tbsp (60 ml) buttermilk

¾ stick (85 g) butter, room temperature, cut in small pieces

Fresh strawberries

Place the egg yolks and sugar in a bowl. Split the vanilla bean and scrape the seeds out, add them to the eggs. Whisk until light and fluffy (I recommend using an electric mixer). Gently fold in the buttermilk, yogurt, lemon juice and zest. Store in the refrigerator until ready to serve.

Preheat the oven to 400°F (200°C). Line a baking sheet with parchment paper.

Stir the flour, baking powder, sugar, vanilla bean, lemon zest and cardamom together in a big bowl.

Add the egg, buttermilk and butter pieces. Use your hands and fingers to knead and pinch the dough together in the bowl. It will come together quickly and easily.

Form small balls (using approximately ½ teaspoon of dough per ball) and place on the baking sheet and bake for 10 minutes. Remove from the oven. When cool enough to handle, cut the cookies in two (horizontally) and lay, cut side up, on the baking sheet. Turn the oven down to 375°F (190°C) and bake for 10 more minutes.

Let cool completely before storing in an airtight container.

Serve the koldskål ice cold. Add fresh strawberries and crumbled kammerjunker on top.

ÆBLESKIVER

A round buttermilk doughnut pancake anyone? This is a true Danish Christmas classic that can easily be enjoyed all year round. I highly recommend making a double recipe and then storing some in the freezer for unexpected guests. Simply heat them up in the oven and they will stay crispy on the outside and soft on the inside.

Fun fact: The translation for æbleskiver is apple slices, but there are no apples involved at all!

YIELD: 14 SERVINGS

1 cup (125 g) flour

2 tsp sugar

½ tsp baking soda

¼ tsp cardamom, ground

2 eggs

1 cup (250 ml) buttermilk

½ vanilla bean

¼ tsp lemon zest

2 tbsp (30 g) butter, melted + more for greasing the pan

Powdered sugar, jam or applesauce for serving

Stir together the flour, sugar, baking soda and cardamom.

Separate the eggs.

In a separate bowl, whisk the egg yolks, buttermilk, seeds from the vanilla bean and lemon zest together. Add to the dry ingredients and whisk fiercely until completely incorporated and smooth, then add melted butter and mix again.

Whisk the whites until completely stiff then fold gently into the dough.

Transfer the dough to a pitcher or other container that is easy to pour from (you could also use a piping bag).

Heat an æbleskiver pan (see Note) on the stove at medium heat and grease each hole with butter. Fill each hole in the pan three-quarters full and when the dough starts to rise and you can see the edges have crisped up, use a chopstick or a knitting needle to turn the half ball a quarter of a turn. Keep turning in quarter turns until you have a whole ball.

Serve piping hot with powdered sugar and jam or applesauce.

NOTE: For more information on frying, there are several videos on YouTube. Cast-iron æbleskiver pans are available in stores and online. If you do not have an æbleskiver pan you can bake the æbleskiver in a muffin tin at 430°F (220°C) for 20 minutes.

DANISH STRAWBERRY TART

WITH MARZIPAN AND CHOCOLATE

You will find a strawberry tart at every bakery in Denmark. They are so popular and when strawberry season hits, Danes are busy baking these babies.

If you do not like marzipan or haven't had it before, this is a great segue to learning to love it. With the chocolate, crème pâtissière and the strawberries, the marzipan is nicely hidden and complements the other ingredients beautifully.

YIELD: 6 SMALL TARTS, OR 1 (8-INCH [20-CM]) LARGE TART

CRÈME PÂTISSIÈRE

1 vanilla bean

¼ cup (50 g) sugar, divided

3 tbsp cornstarch

1¼ cups (300 ml) whole milk, divided

3 egg yolks

1 cup (250 ml) heavy cream

Scrape the seeds out of the vanilla bean onto a cutting board, then sprinkle ½ a tablespoon of the sugar over the seeds. Use the flat side of a knife blade to press down, separating the vanilla seeds and mixing well with the sugar. Then stir together with the remaining sugar in a small bowl and set aside.

In another bowl, dissolve the cornstarch in ¼ cup (60 ml) of the milk then add the egg yolks and vanilla sugar. Whisk together until there are no lumps.

Pour the remaining milk into a saucepan together with the empty vanilla pod over medium heat until the milk is almost boiling, then add the milk/yolk/sugar mixture in a steady stream, whisking constantly. Bring to a boil and let cook until thick. Stir constantly so that the mixture doesn't burn. When it has thickened, taste it to make sure that the cornstarch flavor is gone. If it still tastes floury, cook it 1 to 2 minutes more.

Pour the mixture into a clean bowl and cover with plastic wrap, pressing the plastic wrap directly onto the surface of the pastry cream to prevent a skin from forming. Chill in the refrigerator for 2 hours or up to 2 days. Just before you are ready to put the tart together, whisk the pastry cream until completely smooth then gradually add the heavy cream and whip until smooth.

(continued)

DANISH STRAWBERRY TART

WITH MARZIPAN AND CHOCOLATE (CONTINUED)

TART SHELL

1½ cups (185 g) flour

1 tsp salt

3 tbsp (30 g) powdered sugar

1 stick (115 g) ice-cold butter, cut into cubes

2 egg yolks

FILLING

3.5 oz (100 g) marzipan, grated

3.5 oz (100 g) sugar

2 eggs

¾ stick (85 g) butter, room temperature, cut into small pieces

⅓ cup (40 g) flour

EXTRA

1 oz (30 g) dark chocolate

Fresh strawberries

Preheat the oven to 375°F (190°C).

Place flour, salt and powdered sugar in a food processor. While pulsing, add the ice-cold butter through the feeder tube. Pulse until the dough has a coarse, sand-like texture, then add the yolks and pulse until the dough comes together. Remove the dough from the processor, press it together with your fingers into a ball, wrap in plastic wrap and place in the refrigerator for 1 hour.

Divide the dough into six pieces (if making small tarts) and roll each out into a circle. Press into the six small tart pans or one 8-inch (20-cm) tart pan, prick with a fork a few times and bake for 5 minutes. Remove from the oven and set aside until ready to fill with marzipan.

While the tart is baking, whisk together the grated marzipan, sugar and eggs until the sugar has dissolved. While continuing to whisk, slowly add the butter and continue whisking until fluffy. Fold in the flour until completely combined. Spread the marzipan mixture into the prebaked tart shell (or divide the marzipan mixture between the prebaked tart shells) and bake for 15 to 18 minutes.

Melt the chocolate over a warm-water bath or in a double boiler. When it is melted, use a pastry brush to paint chocolate on top of the tart. Let it cool completely. Place a dollop of pastry cream on top and decorate with strawberries.

ABOUT THE AUTHOR

Katrin Björk was born in Akureyri, Iceland and moved to Copenhagen, Denmark as a 20-year-old to study photography. Katrin pursued a career in Copenhagen as a food and lifestyle photographer before moving with her husband, Jens, and their son, Normann Prince, to New York's Hudson Valley in 2016.

You can see Katrin's photography and find her recipes in well-known magazines and publications such as *Elle Decor, Veranda, Martha Stewart, Wine Enthusiast, Monocle* and the Huffington Post.

Katrín is a self-taught cook who, with her love and passion for food and photography, launched the food blog Modern Wifestyle in 2011.

From the North is Katrin's first book.

Follow her journey at modernwifestyle.com or on Instragram @katrinbjork.

Please use #fromthenorthbook if you decide to publish a picture of the food you cooked from this book.

ACKNOWLEDGMENTS

Endless thanks to my husband, Jens, and our son, Normann Prince, for your never-ending support and patience, for tasting every single recipe in this book and for encouraging me when things tasted good and when they ended up in the trash.

Thank you Mamma and Stefán for being my biggest cheerleaders and for all your support and help.

Thanks to my sister Linda, for your support and for being the most efficient dishwasher during my shoot in Iceland.

Thank you Svanfríður for coming to New York from Iceland to babysit so I could power through and finish the book on time.

Thank you, Guðjón, Lesly and Andrew, Dís and Kasper, for recipe testing and giving me ruthless and honest feedback.

To Þórhildur and Svenni for the eggs, reindeer and kitchen use.

Thanks Þórunn for the beautiful whole, wild salmon.

To Svana and Danni for the goose and ptarmigan—I know it wasn't easy to find wild birds in May and I am forever grateful.

Heiða and Heiða, thanks for the berries.

Thank you Guðrún for the rhubarb.

Big thank you to Aðalsteinn, the priest in Grundarfjörður and to Rúna, Tommi and Unnsteinn for sending me a box filled with wild eggs from Melrakkaey.

The ceramics shown in the photographs in this book were generously lent, given and sold to me by:

- Guðbjörg Káradóttir

- Ólöf Jakobína Ernudóttir at Postulína

- Kristbjörg Guðmundsdóttir

- Lindsey Wohlgemuth at Foxwares

- Breiðfjörð Design

Thank you from the bottom of my heart, Íslensk Hollusta, for your products and inspiration.

Big thanks to Lodge for the æbleskiver pan.

Thank you Einstök beer for sending me the taste of home.

Tinna and Telma, thank you for the Varpið egg necklace I am sporting in my author picture.

Huge thanks to Brit and Shane for listening to me rant about the making of this book. And for always bringing wine.

Last but not least, thank you Page Street Publishing for believing in me and helping me set sail on the wild ocean of cookbooks.

INDEX

A

Æbleskiver, 181
ale, for Blue Mussels with Beer, 46
almonds
  Apple Porridge with Nordic Dukkah,
    166
  Rack of Lamb with Seaweed and
    Almond Crust, 65
  Ramps Pesto, 140
  Reindeer Tartare with Crowberries,
    54
  Smoked Almonds, 123
appetizers
  Arctic Char Tartare, 12
  Pacific Oysters with Blueberry
    Mignonette, 19
  Roasted Beets with Liquorice, 89
  Scallop Ceviche with Elderflower, 15
apples
  Apple Porridge with Nordic Dukkah,
    166
  Birch Granita with Pickled
    Blueberries and Rhubarb
    Foam, 173
  Fresh Potato Salad with Apples and
    Sprouts, 97
  Lamb Chops with Lovage and
    Ramps, 62
  Lobster Roll with Fennel Slaw, 23–25
  Red Cabbage and Apple Slaw with
    Walnuts and Pomegranate,
    105
  Reindeer Tartare with Crowberries,
    54
  Whole Roasted Goose with Prunes,
    Apples and Cinnamon, 80
Arctic Char Tartare, 12
asparagus, for Grilled Asparagus with
    Wild Egg and Sea Truffle, 98

B

bacon
  Liver Paté, 144
  Pheasant with Quince and Bacon, 76
Baked Cod with Fennel and Foam, 37
Baked Leeks with Rosehip and
    Toasted Barley, 90
barley, for Baked Leeks with Rosehip
    and Toasted Barley, 90
beer
  Blue Mussels with Beer, 46
  Fried Cod Cheeks with Baked Root
    Vegetable Crisps, 29

beets
  Cured Trout with Beetroot and
    Birch, 111
  Fried Cod Cheeks with Baked Root
    Vegetable Crisps, 29
  Monkfish with Beet Dressing, 42
  Pickled Beets, 136
  Roasted Beets with Liquorice, 89
  Spicy Kohlrabi and Beets, 101
birch flakes
  Birch Granita with Pickled
    Blueberries and Rhubarb
    Foam, 173
  Blueberry Jam with Birch, 131
  Cured Trout with Beetroot and
    Birch, 111
  Smoked Butter, 119
  Smoked Red Currants, 124
  Smoked Skyr, 120
birch sawdust, for Smoked Almonds,
    123
blackberries, for Night Salted Cod with
    Grilled Cucumber and Fava
    Beans, 33
blackcurrant cordial, for Duck Breast
    with Crispy Skin and Spiced
    Red Cabbage, 71–72
Blistered Radishes with Pickled
    Ramps, 86
blueberries
  Birch Granita with Pickled
    Blueberries and Rhubarb
    Foam, 173
  Blueberry Jam with Birch, 131
  Blueberry Soup, 165
  Chocolate and Caramel Tart with
    Skyr, 170
  Cured Goose Breast with Blueberry
    Dressing, 116
  Icelandic Skyr Cake, 161
  Pacific Oysters with Blueberry
    Mignonette, 19
  Panfried Flounder with Berry Butter
    and Herbs, 34
Blue Mussels with Beer, 46
breads
  Danish Rye Bread, 155
  Sourdough Loaf in Dutch Oven,
    151–152
  Sourdough Pizza, 156
  Sourdough Starter, 149–150
Broth of Lamb with Rutabaga, 53
Brussels sprouts
  Brussels Sprouts with Smoked
    Butter and Sage, 93

  Sourdough Pizza, 156
butter, as Smoked Butter, 119
buttermilk
  Æbleskiver, 181
  Koldskål and Kammerjunker, 178

C

cabbage, green, for Charred Green
    Cabbage with Raspberry
    Vinaigrette, 106
cabbage, red
  Duck Breast with Crispy Skin and
    Spiced Red Cabbage, 71–72
  Red Cabbage and Apple Slaw with
    Walnuts and Pomegranate,
    105
cake
  The Grown-Up Cake with Dates and
    Hazelnuts, 174
  Icelandic Skyr Cake, 161
carrots
  Broth of Lamb with Rutabaga, 53
  Icelandic Langoustine Bisque with
    Cognac, 49
cauliflower, for Icelandic Fishcakes
    with Cauliflower, 30
celeriac, for Stuffed Pork Tenderloin
    with Celery and Hazelnuts, 79
celery
  Grilled Whole Snapper, 41
  Icelandic Langoustine Bisque with
    Cognac, 49
  Stuffed Pork Tenderloin with Celery
    and Hazelnuts, 79
celery leaves
  Crushed Potatoes with Horseradish
    and Duck Fat, 94
  Icelandic Fishcakes with Cauliflower,
    30
Charred Green Cabbage with
    Raspberry Vinaigrette, 106
chive blossoms, as Fried Chive
    Blossoms, 85
chocolate
  Chocolate and Caramel Tart with
    Skyr, 170
  Danish Strawberry Tart with
    Marzipan and Chocolate,
    182–184
  Flødeboller, 177
  The Grown-Up Cake with Dates and
    Hazelnuts, 174
  Icelandic Skyr Cake, 161

coconut
Flødeboller, 177
The Grown-Up Cake with Dates and
Hazelnuts, 174
cod
Baked Cod with Fennel and Foam,
37
Fried Cod Cheeks with Baked Root
Vegetable Crisps, 29
Icelandic Fishcakes with Cauliflower,
30
Night Salted Cod with Grilled
Cucumber and Fava Beans, 33
Pan-Fried Haddock with Rosemary
and Rhubarb, 38
cognac
Blue Mussels with Beer, 46
Icelandic Langoustine Bisque with
Cognac, 49
Comté, for Kräftskive (Crayfish Party),
20–22
cottage cheese, for Blistered Radishes
with Pickled Ramps, 86
cracked rye, for Danish Rye Bread, 155
crayfish, for Kräftskive (Crayfish
Party), 20–22
Crispy Flounder with Sweet Onions on
Danish Rye, 26
crowberries, for Reindeer Tartare with
Crowberries, 54
Crushed Potatoes with Horseradish
and Duck Fat, 94
cucumber
Arctic Char Tartare, 12
Monkfish with Beet Dressing, 42
Night Salted Cod with Grilled
Cucumber and Fava Beans, 33
Scallop Ceviche with Elderflower, 15
Cured Egg Yolks Two Ways, 115
Cured Goose Breast with Blueberry
Dressing, 116
Cured Trout with Beetroot and Birch,
111
currants
Leg of Lamb with Rosemary, Garlic
and Berry Marinade, 61
Panfried Flounder with Berry Butter
and Herbs, 34
Rømmegrøt with Lavender and
Smoked Currants, 162
Smoked Red Currants, 124

D
Danish Crackling Pork with
Sugar-Glazed Potatoes, 69–70
Danish Strawberry Tart with Marzipan
and Chocolate, 182–184
dates
The Grown-Up Cake with Dates and
Hazelnuts, 174
Pheasant with Quince and Bacon, 76

desserts
Æbleskiver, 181
Birch Granita with Pickled
Blueberries and Rhubarb
Foam, 173
Blueberry Soup, 165
Chocolate and Caramel Tart with
Skyr, 170
Danish Strawberry Tart with
Marzipan and Chocolate,
182–184
Flødeboller, 177
The Grown-Up Cake with Dates and
Hazelnuts, 174
Icelandic Skyr Cake, 161
Koldskål and Kammerjunker, 178
Liquorice Ice Cream, 169
Rømmegrøt with Lavender and
Smoked Currants, 162
digestive biscuits, for Icelandic Skyr
Cake, 161
Dijon mustard
Crispy Flounder with Sweet Onions
on Danish Rye, 26
Fresh Potato Salad with Apples and
Sprouts, 97
Graflax (Cured Salmon) with
Mustard Sauce, 112
Kräftskive (Crayfish Party), 20–22
Duck Breast with Crispy Skin and
Spiced Red Cabbage, 71–72
duck fat
Crushed Potatoes with Horseradish
and Duck Fat, 94
Duck Breast with Crispy Skin and
Spiced Red Cabbage, 71
dukkah, for Apple Porridge with
Nordic Dukkah, 166
dulse
Lamb Liver with Dulse "Bacon," 58
Marinated Dulse (Seaweed), 139
Rack of Lamb with Seaweed and
Almond Crust, 65

E
eggs
Æbleskiver, 181
Chocolate and Caramel Tart with
Skyr, 170
Crispy Flounder with Sweet Onions
on Danish Rye, 26
Cured Egg Yolks Two Ways, 115
Danish Strawberry Tart with
Marzipan and Chocolate,
182–184
Flødeboller, 177
Grilled Asparagus with Wild Egg and
Sea Truffle, 98
Grilled Wild Coldwater Shrimp with
Hazelnut Mayonnaise, 16
The Grown-Up Cake with Dates and
Hazelnuts, 174

Icelandic Fishcakes with Cauliflower,
30
Icelandic Skyr Cake, 161
Koldskål and Kammerjunker, 178
Kräftskive (Crayfish Party), 20–22
Liquorice Ice Cream, 169
Liver Paté, 144
Lobster Roll with Fennel Slaw, 23
Reindeer Meatballs with Mushrooms,
57
egg yolks, cured
Cured Egg Yolks Two Ways, 115
Spring Salad with Ramps and Herbs,
102
Einstök White Ale, for Blue Mussels
with Beer, 46
elderflower cordial, for Scallop
Ceviche with Elderflower, 15

F
fava beans, for Night Salted Cod with
Grilled Cucumber and Fava
Beans, 33
fennel
Arctic Char Tartare, 12
Baked Cod with Fennel and Foam,
37
Blue Mussels with Beer, 46
Crispy Flounder with Sweet Onions
on Danish Rye, 26
Lobster Roll with Fennel Slaw, 23–25
feta cheese, for Crushed Potatoes with
Horseradish and Duck Fat, 94
fish stock, for Icelandic Langoustine
Bisque with Cognac, 49
flax seeds, for Danish Rye Bread, 155
Flødeboller, 177
flounder
Crispy Flounder with Sweet Onions
on Danish Rye, 26
Pan-Fried Flounder with Berry
Butter and Herbs, 34
Fresh Potato Salad with Apples and
Sprouts, 97
Fried Chive Blossoms, 85
Fried Cod Cheeks with Baked Root
Vegetable Crisps, 29

G
garlic
Blue Mussels with Beer, 46
Icelandic Langoustine Bisque with
Cognac, 49
Lamb Chops with Lovage and
Ramps, 62
Leg of Lamb with Rosemary, Garlic
and Berry Marinade, 61
Lobster Roll with Fennel Slaw, 23–25
Marinated Dulse (Seaweed), 139
Night Salted Cod with Grilled
Cucumber and Fava Beans, 33

Pan-Fried Flounder with Berry
Butter and Herbs, 34
Reindeer Meatballs with Mushrooms,
57
ginger, for Marinated Dulse (Seaweed),
139
goose breast, as Cured Goose Breast
with Blueberry Dressing, 116
goose, whole, as Whole Roasted
Goose with Prunes, Apples
and Cinnamon, 80
Graflax (Cured Salmon) with Mustard
Sauce, 112
Grilled Asparagus with Wild Egg and
Sea Truffle, 98
Grilled Salmon Steaks with Pickled
Lovage, 45
Grilled Whole Snapper, 41
Grilled Wild Coldwater Shrimp with
Hazelnut Mayonnaise, 16
The Grown-Up Cake with Dates and
Hazelnuts, 174
Gruyère, for Kräftskive (Crayfish
Party), 20–22

H
haddock, as Pan-Fried Haddock with
Rosemary and Rhubarb, 38
hazelnuts
Grilled Wild Coldwater Shrimp with
Hazelnut Mayonnaise, 16
Spicy Kohlrabi and Beets, 101
Stuffed Pork Tenderloin with Celery
and Hazelnuts, 79
heavy cream
Blueberry Soup, 165
Chocolate and Caramel Tart with
Skyr, 170
Danish Strawberry Tart with
Marzipan and Chocolate,
182–184
The Grown-Up Cake with Dates and
Hazelnuts, 174
Icelandic Langoustine Bisque with
Cognac, 49
Icelandic Skyr Cake, 161
Liquorice Ice Cream, 169
Reindeer Meatballs with Mushrooms,
57
honey
Fresh Potato Salad with Apples and
Sprouts, 97
Graflax (Cured Salmon) with
Mustard Sauce, 112
Monkfish with Beet Dressing, 42
Roasted Beets with Liquorice, 89
horseradish, for Crushed Potatoes with
Horseradish and Duck Fat, 94

I
ice cream, as Liquorice Ice Cream, 169
Icelandic Fishcakes with Cauliflower,
30
Icelandic Langoustine Bisque with
Cognac, 49
Icelandic Skyr Cake, 161

J
jam
Æbleskiver, 181
Blueberry Jam with Birch, 131
Cured Goose Breast with Blueberry
Dressing, 116
Reindeer Meatballs with Mushrooms,
57
juniper berries
Pheasant with Quince and Bacon, 76
Preserved Pears, 132
Reindeer Meatballs with Mushrooms,
57
Reindeer Tartare with Crowberries,
54

K
Kahlua, for Chocolate and Caramel
Tart with Skyr, 170
Kammerjunker, 178
kohlrabi, for Spicy Kohlrabi and Beets,
101
Koldskål and Kammerjunker, 178
Kräftskiva (Crayfish Party), 20–22

L
Lamb Chops with Lovage and Ramps,
62
lamb, leg of, as Leg of Lamb with
Rosemary, Garlic and Berry
Marinade, 61
Lamb Liver with Dulse "Bacon," 58
lamb, rack of, as Rack of Lamb with
Seaweed and Almond Crust,
65
lamb shoulder, for Broth of Lamb with
Rutabaga, 53
langoustine, as Icelandic Langoustine
Bisque with Cognac, 49
lavender blossoms, for Rømmegrøt
with Lavender and Smoked
Currants, 162
leeks
Baked Leeks with Rosehip and
Toasted Barley, 90
Broth of Lamb with Rutabaga, 53
Leg of Lamb with Rosemary, Garlic
and Berry Marinade, 61
lemon juice
Arctic Char Tartare, 12
Birch Granita with Pickled
Blueberries and Rhubarb
Foam, 173

Blistered Radishes with Pickled
Ramps, 86
Crushed Potatoes with Horseradish
and Duck Fat, 94
Flødeboller, 177
Fried Cod Cheeks with Baked Root
Vegetable Crisps, 29
Grilled Wild Coldwater Shrimp with
Hazelnut Mayonnaise, 16
Koldskål and Kammerjunker, 178
Kräftskive (Crayfish Party), 20–22
Lamb Liver with Dulse "Bacon," 58
Leg of Lamb with Rosemary, Garlic
and Berry Marinade, 61
Lobster Roll with Fennel Slaw, 23–25
Monkfish with Beet Dressing, 42
Ramps Pesto, 140
lemon slices, for Grilled Whole
Snapper, 41
lemon zest
Æbleskiver, 181
Arctic Char Tartare, 12
Fried Cod Cheeks with Baked Root
Vegetable Crisps, 29
Koldskål and Kammerjunker, 178
Leg of Lamb with Rosemary, Garlic
and Berry Marinade, 61
Rhubarb Syrup and Compote, 135
lime juice
Roasted Beets with Liquorice, 89
Scallop Ceviche with Elderflower, 15
Spicy Kohlrabi and Beets, 101
Liquorice Ice Cream, 169
liver
Lamb Liver with Dulse "Bacon," 58
Liver Paté, 144
Lobster Roll with Fennel Slaw, 23–25
lovage
Lamb Chops with Lovage and
Ramps, 62
Spring Salad with Ramps and Herbs,
102

M
mackerel, as Smoked Mackerel, 127
maple syrup
Brussels Sprouts with Smoked
Butter and Sage, 93
Whole Roasted Goose with Prunes,
Apples and Cinnamon, 80
maple wood shavings
Smoked Almonds, 123
Smoked Butter, 119
Smoked Skyr, 120
Marinated Dulse (Seaweed), 139
marzipan, for Danish Strawberry Tart
with Marzipan and Chocolate,
182–184
mayonnaise
Hazelnut Mayonnaise, 16
Kräftskive, 20–22

meatballs, as Reindeer Meatballs with Mushrooms, 57
metric measurements, 9
milk
  Baked Cod with Fennel and Foam, 37
  Chocolate and Caramel Tart with Skyr, 170
  Danish Strawberry Tart with Marzipan and Chocolate, 182–184
  Icelandic Skyr Cake, 161
  Liquorice Ice Cream, 169
  Liver Paté, 144
  Night Salted Cod with Grilled Cucumber and Fava Beans, 33
  Rømmegrøt with Lavender and Smoked Currants, 162
Monkfish with Beet Dressing, 42
mozzarella cheese, for Sourdough Pizza, 156
mushrooms, for Reindeer Meatballs with Mushrooms, 57
mussels, as Blue Mussels with Beer, 46
mustard
  Crispy Flounder with Sweet Onions on Danish Rye, 26
  Fresh Potato Salad with Apples and Sprouts, 97
  Graflax (Cured Salmon) with Mustard Sauce, 112
  Kräftskive (Crayfish Party), 20–22
  Red Cabbage and Apple Slaw with Walnuts and Pomegranate, 105

N
Night Salted Cod with Grilled Cucumber and Fava Beans, 33

O
onions, red
  Lamb Liver with Dulse "Bacon," 58
  Monkfish with Beet Dressing, 42
  Rock Ptarmigan with Vanilla, 66
  Stuffed Pork Tenderloin with Celery and Hazelnuts, 79
onions, yellow
  Crispy Flounder with Sweet Onions on Danish Rye, 26
  Icelandic Langoustine Bisque with Cognac, 49
  Icelandic Fishcakes with Cauliflower, 30
  Liver Paté, 144
  Reindeer Meatballs with Mushrooms, 57
  Sourdough Pizza, 156
  Whole Roasted Goose with Prunes, Apples and Cinnamon, 80

orange, diced, for Duck Breast with Crispy Skin and Spiced Red Cabbage, 71–72
orange juice, for Charred Green Cabbage with Raspberry Vinaigrette, 106
oysters, as Pacific Oysters with Blueberry Mignonette, 19

P
Pacific Oysters with Blueberry Mignonette, 19
Pan-Fried Flounder with Berry Butter and Herbs, 34
Pan-Fried Haddock with Rosemary and Rhubarb, 38
Parmesan cheese, for Ramps Pesto, 140
parsley
  Blue Mussels with Beer, 46
  Brussels Sprouts with Smoked Butter and Sage, 93
  Crushed Potatoes with Horseradish and Duck Fat, 94
  Fresh Potato Salad with Apples and Sprouts, 97
  Icelandic Langoustine Bisque with Cognac, 49
  Monkfish with Beet Dressing, 42
  Pacific Oysters with Blueberry Mignonette, 19
  Red Cabbage and Apple Slaw with Walnuts and Pomegranate, 105
  Reindeer Tartare with Crowberries, 54
parsnips
  Broth of Lamb with Rutabaga, 53
  Lamb Liver with Dulse "Bacon," 58
paté, as Liver Paté, 144
pears, as Preserved Pears, 132
pesto, as Ramps Pesto, 140
Pheasant with Quince and Bacon, 76
Pickled Beets, 136
Pickled Ramps, 143
pizza, as Sourdough Pizza, 156
pomegranate, for Red Cabbage and Apple Slaw with Walnuts and Pomegranate, 105
pork fat, for Liver Paté, 144
pork liver, for Liver Paté, 144
pork roast, for Danish Crackling Pork with Sugar-Glazed Potatoes, 69–70
pork tenderloin, for Stuffed Pork Tenderloin with Celery and Hazelnuts, 79
porridge, for Apple Porridge with Nordic Dukkah, 166
potatoes
  Crushed Potatoes with Horseradish and Duck Fat, 94

Danish Crackling Pork with Sugar-Glazed Potatoes, 69–70
  Fresh Potato Salad with Apples and Sprouts, 97
Preserved Pears, 132
prunes
  Rock Ptarmigan with Vanilla, 66
  Whole Roasted Goose with Prunes, Apples and Cinnamon, 80
pumpkin seeds, for Danish Rye Bread, 155

Q
quince, for Pheasant with Quince and Bacon, 76

R
Rack of Lamb with Seaweed and Almond Crust, 65
radishes
  Blistered Radishes with Pickled Ramps, 86
  Crispy Flounder with Sweet Onions on Danish Rye, 26
  Fresh Potato Salad with Apples and Sprouts, 97
  Monkfish with Beet Dressing, 42
ramps
  Blistered Radishes with Pickled Ramps, 86
  Lamb Chops with Lovage and Ramps, 62
  Pickled Ramps, 143
  Ramps Pesto, 140
  Spring Salad with Ramps and Herbs, 102
raspberries
  Charred Green Cabbage with Raspberry Vinaigrette, 106
  Panfried Flounder with Berry Butter and Herbs, 34
Red Cabbage and Apple Slaw with Walnuts and Pomegranate, 105
red currants
  Whole Roasted Goose with Prunes, Apples and Cinnamon, 80
reindeer
  Reindeer Meatballs with Mushrooms, 57
  Reindeer Tartare with Crowberries, 54
rhubarb
  Birch Granita with Pickled Blueberries and Rhubarb Foam, 173
  The Grown-Up Cake with Dates and Hazelnuts, 174
  Pan-Fried Haddock with Rosemary and Rhubarb, 38
  Rhubarb Syrup and Compote, 135

Roasted Beets with Liquorice, 89
Rock Ptarmigan with Vanilla, 66
Rømmegrøt with Lavender and
    Smoked Currants, 162
rosehips, for Baked Leeks with Rosehip
    and Toasted Barley, 90
rutabaga
    Broth of Lamb with Rutabaga, 53
    Fried Cod Cheeks with Baked Root
        Vegetable Crisps, 29
rye bread
    Crispy Flounder with Sweet Onions
        on Danish Rye, 26
    Danish Rye Bread, 155
    Grilled Asparagus with Wild Egg and
        Sea Truffle, 98

S
sage
    Brussels Sprouts with Smoked
        Butter and Sage, 93
    Spring Salad with Ramps and Herbs,
        102
salads
    Fresh Potato Salad with Apples and
        Sprouts, 97
    Spicy Kohlrabi and Beets, 101
    Spring Salad with Ramps and Herbs,
        102
salmon
    Graflax (Cured Salmon) with
        Mustard Sauce, 112
    Grilled Salmon Steaks with Pickled
        Lovage, 45
sawdust, for Smoked Almonds, 123
Scallop Ceviche with Elderflower, 15
sea truffles, for Grilled Asparagus with
    Wild Egg and Sea Truffle, 98
seaweed
    Grilled Asparagus with Wild Egg and
        Sea Truffle, 98
    Lamb Liver with Dulse "Bacon," 58
    Marinated Dulse (Seaweed), 139
    Rack of Lamb with Seaweed and
        Almond Crust, 65
shallots
    Blue Mussels with Beer, 46
    Charred Green Cabbage with
        Raspberry Vinaigrette, 106
    Pacific Oysters with Blueberry
        Mignonette, 19
    Reindeer Tartare with Crowberries,
        54
shrimp, as Grilled Wild Coldwater
    Shrimp with Hazelnut
    Mayonnaise, 16
sides
    Baked Leeks with Rosehip and
        Toasted Barley, 90
    Blistered Radishes with Pickled
        Ramps, 86

Brussels Sprouts with Smoked
    Butter and Sage, 93
Charred Green Cabbage with
    Raspberry Vinaigrette, 106
Crushed Potatoes with Horseradish
    and Duck Fat, 94
Fried Chive Blossoms, 85
Grilled Asparagus with Wild Egg and
    Sea Truffle, 98
Roasted Beets with Liquorice, 89
skyr
    Chocolate and Caramel Tart with
        Skyr, 170
    Crushed Potatoes with Horseradish
        and Duck Fat, 94
    Fried Cod Cheeks with Baked Root
        Vegetable Crisps, 29
    Icelandic Skyr Cake, 161
    Lobster Roll with Fennel Slaw, 23–25
    Monkfish with Beet Dressing, 42
    Smoked Skyr, 120
Smoked Almonds, 123
Smoked Butter, 119
Smoked Mackerel, 127
Smoked Red Currants, 124
Smoked Skyr, 120
snapper, for Grilled Whole Snapper, 41
sour cream
    Baked Cod with Fennel and Foam,
        37
    Fresh Potato Salad with Apples and
        Sprouts, 97
    Graflax (Cured Salmon) with
        Mustard Sauce, 112
    Pan-Fried Flounder with Berry
        Butter and Herbs, 34
    Rømmegrøt with Lavender and
        Smoked Currants, 162
sourdough bread
    Grilled Wild Coldwater Shrimp with
        Hazelnut Mayonnaise, 16
    Kräftskive (Crayfish Party), 20–22
    Sourdough Loaf in Dutch Oven,
        151–152
    Sourdough Pizza, 156
    Sourdough Starter, 149–150
Spicy Kohlrabi and Beets, 101
Spring Salad with Ramps and Herbs,
    102
strawberries
    Danish Strawberry Tart with
        Marzipan and Chocolate,
        182–184
    The Grown-Up Cake with Dates and
        Hazelnuts, 174
    Koldskål and Kammerjunker, 178
    Spicy Kohlrabi and Beets, 101
    Stuffed Pork Tenderloin with Celery
        and Hazelnuts, 79
sugar snap peas
    Sourdough Pizza, 156

Spring Salad with Ramps and Herbs,
    102
sunchokes
    Lobster Roll with Fennel Slaw, 23–25
    Veal Chops with Sunchoke Purée, 75
sunflower seeds, for Danish Rye Bread,
    155

T
tartare
    Arctic Char Tartare, 12
    Reindeer Tartare with Crowberries,
        54
tarts
    Chocolate and Caramel Tart with
        Skyr, 170
    Danish Strawberry Tart with
        Marzipan and Chocolate,
        182–184
tenderloin, as Stuffed Pork Tenderloin
    with Celery and Hazelnuts, 79
tomato paste, for Icelandic
    Langoustine Bisque with
    Cognac, 49
trout, as Cured Trout with Beetroot
    and Birch, 111

V
Veal Chops with Sunchoke Purée, 75
venison
    Reindeer Meatballs with Mushrooms,
        57
    Reindeer Tartare with Crowberries, 54

W
waffle wafers, for Flødeboller, 177
walnuts
    Red Cabbage and Apple Slaw with
        Walnuts and Pomegranate,
        105
    Reindeer Meatballs with Mushrooms,
        57
watercress, for Spicy Kohlrabi and
    Beets, 101
white ale, for Blue Mussels with Beer,
    46
white chocolate, for Chocolate and
    Caramel Tart with Skyr, 170
Whole Roasted Goose with Prunes,
    Apples and Cinnamon, 80
wood shavings and sawdust
    Smoked Almonds, 123
    Smoked Butter, 119
    Smoked Mackerel, 127
    Smoked Red Currants, 124
    Smoked Skyr, 120

Y
yogurt, for Koldskål and
    Kammerjunker, 178